Duru Indi

My Transformative Guide

JASMINE HONG

Copyright © 2021 Jasmine Hong

All rights reserved. No part of this publication may be reproduced or transmitted in any form or by any means, electronic or mechanical, including photocopy, recording, or any information storage and retrieval system, without permission in writing from the publisher.

Printed in the United States.

Cover and book design by Asya Blue Design.
Editors: Jay Mason, Kristin Lin
Proofreader: Shay Maunz

Disclaimer: The contents of this book are not intended to be a substitute for professional medical advice, diagnosis, or treatment. The author is not a doctor or a vet. The author is sharing this information and her experience for educational purposes only. Always seek the advice of a qualified vet or an appropriately qualified healthcare provider for any questions you have regarding a medical condition and before undertaking any diet or other health-related program. Do not disregard the advice of a medical professional or delay in seeking it because of something you have read in this book. If you choose to rely on any information provided in Duru Indi, you do so solely at your own risk. Under no circumstances is the author responsible for the claims of third-party websites or educational providers.

ISBN 978-1-7379907-0-3 Paperback
ISBN 978-1-7379907-2-7 Ebook

*Dedicated to all the lightworkers
quietly working amongst us.*

TABLE OF CONTENTS

Preface 1
Chapter 1   *Indi* 5
Chapter 2   *Heart failure* 11
Chapter 3   *Intuition—knowing without knowing how* 17
Chapter 4   *Déjà vu—one day at a time* 21
Chapter 5   *Repeated patterns* 25
Chapter 6   *New city* 33
Chapter 7   *My emotional compass—Indi's belly* 37
Chapter 8   *Connecting the dots* 45
Chapter 9   *Doing versus being* 47
Chapter 10   *Indi's "voice"* 51
Chapter 11   *Three times, not a charm* 63
Chapter 12   *Seeds of inspiration* 73
Chapter 13   *Nothing is impossible!* 79
Chapter 14   *My transformative guide* 83
Chapter 15   *Bar-hopping!* 87

Chapter 16	*Beautiful death*	91
Chapter 17	*Grief*	101
Chapter 18	*Big D and little d*	107
Chapter 19	*Reflections*	111
Chapter 20	*Journey after the journey*	115

A letter to Indi 119

Further Insights 121

   A. Critical thinking 121

   B. The power of thoughts and prayers 122

   C. Conscious self-care 124

   D. Breathing and meditation 125

   E. The gift of sensitivity 127

   F. Beneficial modalities 129

   G. Other tips 133

Memories of Indi from Christina 139

Notes 141

Web references 143

PREFACE

I never dreamed of writing anything other than what was required of me. In fact, when I was nine years old, I was labeled as "the girl who doesn't like to write."

Growing up in education-mad South Korea required an all-encompassing commitment to education and academic achievements. A near-stifling regimen left little room for self-reflection and the development of one's inner senses. However, the furious pace and expectations forced me to seek an alternative path.

Then, in my 20s, with only rudimentary foreign-language skills, I took a leap of faith and transplanted deep into the heart of Texas to pursue a master's degree in nursing. It was during this period that I came into contact with a being who would forever change my life.

Indi arrived as a 5-pound ball of Cavalier fluff and eventually grew into a 15-pound guru emanating wisdom, strength and pure love.

Despite his diminutive size, Indi's bug eyes could bring a smile to the face of even the toughest critic. He inspired with his tenacity for life and a spirit stronger than any person I've ever known.

"Truly a regal character," described by one of his disciples.

With his undying love, Indi left an indelible mark on my life—and that of my husband.

We welcome animals into our lives thinking that we are their superiors—that we know what's best for all. Naturally, what follows is training and obedience sessions. You know, setting the rules.

I bought into this—at least, in the beginning. But with time, I began to notice peculiar, recurring thoughts about this little guy. When Indi was young, there were times when I had difficulty seeing my own path forward. He often sat down next to me and fixated with a long, unblinking stare. It was as if he wanted to comfort me, to let me know that everything would be OK. In those moments, somehow, this 'trainee' appeared wise beyond his years.

I pondered: *What if pets are here to remind us of what truly matters? Could we learn more about ourselves through their way of being? Can an animal be our teacher?*

Life's hectic pace leads us to focus on externalities, such as material goods, success, and power. We surround ourselves with badges and trophies, believing that striving for more achievements will render greater happiness and fulfillment. As a result, our inner lives suffer, and we lose sight of what is important.

Animals have a closer relationship with nature. They remind us that we are also a part of nature and can lead us to greater insights.

As I fumbled to understand my role in life, Indi was tragically diagnosed with a heart condition. It was during this time that I became sensitized to his efforts to communicate with me. That helped me to grow more aware of my inner voice. It caused me to rethink my priorities and open up to the spiritual side of life.

In his quiet, unassuming ways, Indi became more than a companion. He became my four-legged guru.

During Indi's illness, my inability to articulate unconventional thoughts and feelings often led to communication difficulties. I couldn't stand up for Indi because I struggled to voice my intuitive convictions at critical moments.

These difficulties steered me to the path of cultivation in order to better advocate for the voiceless. For readers who studied in the realms of energy or spirituality, these concepts should already be familiar.

I knew in my heart that it was Indi's wish for me to write this book about our journey. To ensure this idea germinated, he stayed with me for as long as possible. I hope this story inspires others to pursue their own path of growth and that, in turn, they share theirs with the world.

Animals don't come into our lives by accident. In his brief time on this planet, Indi more than proved his worth. His value as a spiritual guide who lovingly taught me to listen to my inner voice: priceless.

"A human being is a part of the whole, called by us 'universe', a part limited in time and space. He experiences himself, his thoughts and feelings as something separated from the rest—a kind of optical delusion of his consciousness. This delusion is a kind of prison for us, restricting us to our personal desires and to affection for a few persons nearest to us. Our task must be to free ourselves from this prison by widening our circle of compassion to embrace all living creatures and the whole of nature in its beauty. Nobody is able to achieve this completely, but the striving for such achievement is in itself a part of the liberation and a foundation for inner security."

—ALBERT EINSTEIN

CHAPTER 1
Indi

"Some of our greatest historical and artistic treasures we place with curators in museums; others we take for walks."

—ROGER A. CARAS

In South Korea, most kids walk to school or take public transportation by themselves. On my first day walking to school at the tender age of 6, I had a traumatizing experience.

About 500 meters from school, I came across a small white dog. I froze. Maybe sensing fear, he barked aggressively and ran towards me. In full flight, he chased me all the way to the school entrance. I cried and remained shaken by this experience for years.

From then on, I even hid at the sight of any passing dog and purposely avoided visiting dog-owning friends. Petting an animal was out of the question—until I met Indi.

Indi was three months old when my then-husband brought him home unexpectedly. I had never wanted a dog. To me, they were scary and needy. An animal in the house was not a pleasant thought. But my husband had quietly plotted behind my back, researching breeds that matched my personality. He later told me that the choice had come down to a Boston Terrier or a Cavalier King Charles Spaniel. He had decided on the latter because of their reputation for being gentle and having a calm demeanor, as well as for being adorable.

My husband acquired Indi from a reputable breeder in San Antonio, Texas. Unbeknownst to me, he had spent six hours that day watching and observing the available puppies. He proclaimed that he had picked the best-behaved one.

On July 3rd, 2007, my husband walked through our front door with a carrier in his hand. I was shocked. But that wasn't all. Since neither of us had any experience with dogs, he had also invited some friends who happened to own four of them. Coincidentally(?), they arrived minutes after Indi's grand entrance. Needless to say, I was upset but didn't have the time or space to express it. Our friends wanted to immediately meet the new puppy.

When my husband let this tiny creature out of his carrier, the smell was so strong that I backed away. Amazingly, in a room with four, he walked straight towards me.

I was not impressed. He was cute, sure, but I just wanted to get away from the smell—and avoid getting bitten. As I retreated, he followed me from room to room, completely ignoring the three actual dog lovers in the house. Our friends told me that this meant Indi had chosen me as his "master."

"What? Why on earth would he choose me?" I had never wanted a dog and certainly didn't know how to care for one, let alone be its master.

Master or not, I couldn't stand his odor. So, I lured him to the bathroom and placed him into the tub. He didn't resist. He was very calm; actually, calmer than me. I didn't know exactly how to wash this little guy and was still worried about being bitten.

In the tub, doused with water, he looked even tinier. Suddenly, I felt sorry that he had been taken from his family and now had to endure bathing in a new place with an inexperienced owner. I was as gentle as possible, understanding how stressful that day's events must have been for him. He was such a gentle boy during the bath, which led me to think he had a very trusting nature. *Were all dogs like him?*

Having arrived the day before the American Independence Day, I hoped his destiny was to be a strong and independent dog[1].

On the first morning, he was wide awake in his carrier, wagging his tail furiously with excitement. I greeted him with a gentle hug and a 'hello' sniff to make him feel safe in his new environment. He greeted me with a lick on my hand. As soon as I put him down, he started to explore the house. We had a two-story home with stairs. Each step was as tall as he was, but Indi didn't hesitate to climb up and down. This tiny guy was braver than he looked. He was patient, attentive, smart—perfect from day one.

---

1   Accordingly, he was named Indi.

Less than 24 hours after our first encounter, I had started to fall for this little guy. From that point on, he was like a fuzzy little shadow.

Although I didn't have a clue how to train a dog, it was darn easy to be his "master." He acted like he knew what to do and how to behave. He was a small, four-legged, classy gentleman.

Yet, to be certain, we did attend an obedience class. Once. As first-time dog owners, my husband and I thought we could learn something from the class. But it didn't take long to realize that Indi was the most well-behaved participant, so we moved on. He was going to be home-schooled or no-schooled.

Indi loved to be with "his" people. He had to know what they were up to, especially me. To keep track of me, he would either put his paw on my leg or his butt near my face when I laid down.

He was a very deep sleeper and, therefore, not much of a guard dog. His skills were of the herding variety. He would often shepherd his people into the same room to keep watch over the 'flock'.

His memory was outstanding. He recognized places after only one visit. One evening, we went out for a stroll and stopped by a shoe store to window shop. A few days later, on another walk, Indi suddenly stopped at the same shoe store and looked at me as if to ask, "Are we going in?"

However, sometimes his memory worked against him.

When I would take my car in for a check-up at the local dealership, Indi would begin shaking uncontrollably. Next door was his vet's office.

He was always very quiet. In fact, he didn't bark until he was 4 years old. It was his first squirrel sighting.

Unfortunately, not long after Indi's arrival, my marriage fell apart. As I was sitting on the patio pondering life's next step, Indi came over, sat next to me and let out a huge sigh. It was as if he understood my concerns and struggles. As he stared into my eyes, I sensed a deeper connection with him, like he was trying to communicate an insight.

Then a strange thought came to me: Maybe Indi and I were meant to be together at this particular time for reasons I didn't quite yet understand.

But I quickly dismissed this as nonsense, thinking, "He's just a dog."

When the divorce was finalized, my ex-husband took Indi. He was the one who had wanted a dog in the first place. I was devastated but reassured that Indi would be in good hands.

I moved to Dallas and continued to work as an acupuncturist. A year and a half later, out of the blue, my ex called me. He had decided to bring Indi back to me. His situation had changed, which meant he couldn't spend much time with Indi anymore. He also warned me that Indi had become untrainable. He was doing his business everywhere but outside.

That was not the Indi I remembered. But I didn't care. I was just happy to have him back in my life.

However, after a year and a half, I worried that Indi wouldn't remember me. But the day we were reunited, our bond was as strong as ever. He was still perfect in every way.

At my workplace, he deservedly earned the title of CCO – Chief Cuddling Officer. We were also travel buddies, roaming between his adoring relatives and friends in the Dallas, Houston, Austin triangle. Needless to say, bug-eye Indi was exceptional at meeting new people and enhancing his mother's social life at the local Starbucks. Several years later, after having met my new husband, Indi went international. My new beau moved us to Edmonton, Canada. Together, Indi and I started a new life there, adventuring into the pristine and majestic Rocky Mountains whenever we could. And even though Indi was born in Texas, on the first snow, he bunny-hopped and yelped with pleasure.

Everything seemed to be working out for us and this new relationship.

CHAPTER 2
Heart failure

"Whatever is rejected from the self, appears in the world as an event."

—CARL JUNG

In September 2013, we headed to Montreal. The architecture reminded me of Europe and the streets were alive with culture. Despite the language barrier, I could feel the kind and joyous nature of the locals. With the onset of a picturesque autumn and perfect weather, we decided to extend our visit for three months to see whether we wanted to settle down in Montreal.

In this new village, Indi developed a peculiar habit. Each morning he would arise early and sit in front of the door, quietly waiting for me to awaken.

He had never been a morning pup until he discovered Mont Royal.

Indi wasn't interested in chasing a ball, swimming, or playing with other dogs. But he loved mountains. When surrounded by trees, he would spend hours gleefully chasing squirrels. (They were either Indi's passion or nemesis—I could never figure it out.)

Our time in Montreal was magical. Though I couldn't speak French, the thought of living there fancied all of us.

One day in early November, the unusual morning chill in the air announced that winter was coming. After our usual romp on Mont Royal, Indi suddenly burst out a single, loud cough. I'd never heard this before. It left me with a weird, nagging feeling that something was not quite right.

At first, we thought he might have a cold. But that night, a realization jerked me awake from a deep sleep.

"Something is wrong with Indi's heart," I muttered.

At 12:43 am, Indi was sleeping peacefully at the foot of the bed, but that sound of his cough kept repeating in my head. His last check-up had been a year earlier. Until this cough, Indi had been very active, but I couldn't shake the feeling that something was seriously wrong.

During the night, I did some research. Unfortunately, there was nothing conclusive. A dog could cough for any number of reasons. But my gut instinct was that it was a heart problem. After reading about a natural approach to treating congestive heart failure, I immediately ordered some products.

At this exploratory stage, my husband and I still weren't sure where we would eventually settle. Equally uncertain was whether to continue my career as an acupuncturist or to explore other options. There was something I was meant to do but didn't know what it was.

For some strange reason, I felt Indi's heart problem might also be linked to my life's path.

In the morning, it felt necessary to take Indi to a local veterinary hospital. In Montreal, we didn't have a regular vet. The only way to see one during the weekend was to take Indi to emergency care, which would be expensive. My husband thought I was overreacting. Indi looked tired and wasn't acting like his usual enthusiastic self, but he didn't look terribly ill, either. He argued that Indi had been healthy up until just yesterday, so jumping to the worst-case scenario was unreasonable. He suggested Indi might simply have a cold due to the sudden drop in temperature. His reasoning made sense.

The conversation got heated. I didn't have a strong, convincing argument to justify spending thousands of dollars on an emergency visit. It was just a gut feeling.

We eventually agreed to make an appointment with a vet as soon as we could instead of taking Indi to the ER that day. The earliest a vet could see Indi was in three days.

I hoped my husband was right, and that Indi had simply taken a cold but couldn't shake the nagging feeling that it was a mistake not to go to the hospital.

How to convince others to take action based on a gut feeling? I faced this challenge many times during my journey with Indi. Yet, looking back, even I wasn't completely convinced. I didn't yet trust my intuition. Before leaping into action, most of us need some form of tangible proof. We often ignore or scoff at feelings and intuition, even if they're our own.

Over the weekend, Indi's condition gradually worsened. He still went outside to relieve himself but lacked his usual enthusiasm. By Monday morning, he was clearly in distress. He was barely able to stand, his breathing had become labored, and even vomited.

At the vet, Indi was examined briefly only to be given an imperative verdict to rush him to the hospital. Although the vet was calm, I could sense the urgency. He called ahead.

Indi looked weak in my arms and getting worse by the minute. Tears streamed down my cheeks. I felt guilty for not having listened to my gut feeling.

When we arrived, the hospital staff were waiting for us. Immediately, they rushed Indi into an oxygen box. My worst fear was confirmed: Indi's heart had failed. Blood had been leaking through the mitral valve and backed up into his lungs. Indi was literally drowning. The vet explained that Indi needed a diuretic to remove the water from his lungs and that they needed to keep him in the hospital until he was stable and able to breathe on his own. She also warned us that Indi might not make it.

No, this can't be right. Indi has to come home with me. We still have work to do, whatever that might be.

That night, around midnight, we got a phone call from the hospital. The vet said that Indi wasn't responding to the diuretic treatment and wanted to increase the dosage. She also mentioned that we might have to prepare ourselves for the worst. Further updates would come.

I was in shock. Just days ago, we were all out romping around.

My throat choked up, and I was barely able to relay the doctor's message to my husband. He held me silently, and I knew he felt terrible too.

I dozed off in front of the phone and awoke at 4 am. Still no word. So, I called the hospital. They reported that Indi was responding to the treatment and his breathing had improved.

Indi would live. Finally, I could breathe.

Two days later he was discharged. Yet, the prognosis was still not good: Indi was not likely to survive more than two years. Of course, I didn't believe it; Indi would be different.

But when the vet brought Indi into the room, doubt crept into my conviction. Indi's eyes were blank. In place of the usual sparkle, there was sheer exhaustion and emptiness, as if surviving had taken every last bit of strength from his body and spirit.

At home, he continued to linger. He needed to rest and to find his own level of activity. Thankfully, about 10 days later that Cavalier vibrancy returned and life seemed to be back to normal again.

What was the most significant change you made after his heart failed? Indi's foods!

After this near-catastrophic heart failure, I researched and consulted with a few homeopathic vets. They explained that dry foods are very taxing to an animal's body. They consume dogs' essential digestive fluids, which are used to rehydrate dry food instead of absorbing nutrition. Over time, dogs not only become dehydrated but also nutritionally deficient. Dry food lacks nutrition because of the manufacturing process. A diet focused on dry food can lead to all kinds of diseases.[2]

In most dry pet foods, regardless of the price, the average starch content is about 40 percent. Starch is included to reduce the cost of production. Just like sugar can harm the human body, many health issues in dogs can be attributed to this hidden carbohydrate in their diets.[3]

Like humans, animals benefit from diverse diets. The Human Microbiome Project, a 10-year research initiative funded by the National Institutes of Health, showed that our body carries 10 times as many microbes as human cells. The more diverse our diet, the more biodiversity there is in our microbiomes, and the healthier we are.

A dogs' gut microbiome health is similar to a human's[4]. This means that what is good for humans will likely be good for animals.

---

2   https://thelightofdog.com/why-dry-kibble-is-bad-for-dogs/
3   The Truth About Pet Cancer, a seven-part docu-series
4   https://microbiomejournal.biomedcentral.com/articles/10.1186/s40168-018-0450-3

CHAPTER 3
Intuition—knowing without knowing how

"The intuitive mind is a sacred gift, and the rational mind is a faithful servant. We have created a society that honors the servant and has forgotten the gift."
—ALBERT EINSTEIN

Listening to my intuition could have saved Indi a lot of grief. Yet, up until this point, I primarily relied on the logical mind and didn't fully trust intuition.

Revolutionary thinkers and artists such as Albert Einstein, Steve Jobs, and Leonardo da Vinci recognized the importance of intuition in their work. They understood that intuition is an essential tool for tapping into the stream of information beyond the limits of what our senses can perceive. However, we rarely talk about the importance of intuition. Naturally, many of us lose touch with it.

Macquarie Dictionary defines the word as the "direct perception of truths, facts, etc., independently of any reasoning process."

The important point is that there is no reasoning process. There is no scientific proof or concrete evidence. It's knowing without knowing how or why.

We rely on intuition more often than we think, especially when we make truly life-changing decisions, like choosing a life partner, family planning or changing jobs. Sometimes intuition saves lives. We've all heard stories of people who sense that something doesn't feel right and avoid a plane crash, for example.

Intuition is a powerful, unseen force guiding us. It is linked to the wisdom of the heart and cosmic intelligence. Yet, at times, following our intuition feels like a fish swimming upstream. It certainly felt that way on this journey with Indi.

Intuitive signals may be confusing and are frequently ignored, but it is ever-present. Where action has been primarily driven by logic and reasoning, learning to trust one's intuition takes time and experience. Rather than dismissing it, when we learn to understand and embrace intuition, it can help in our decision-making process.

Before Indi's sickness, I didn't have much of a relationship with intuition. But after returning home from the hospital, I continued to experience situations where logic failed me. Intuition was being pushed to the forefront. As our journey progressed, this became an invaluable resource.

Learning to listen to my intuition is like having a trusted, invisible ally. It was one of the great lessons from Indi.

Developing a relationship with your intuition

We need to nurture a relationship with our intuition to be able to discern its voice from others. Just like learning any skill, this becomes easier with practice.

The key is learning to quiet the mind and listen to our inner voice. Regularly setting aside alone time, whether to take a bath or spend time in nature, is a good starting point.

Above all, meditation is an effective way to tap into intuition. To cultivate this practice, we don't need an hour, not even 30 minutes. Just 10 minutes every day is fine. (More information about meditation can be found in "Breathing and meditation" at the end of the book.)

The best time to meditate is early in the morning, right after waking, when the world is still quiet with sleep. But it can be done any time of the day. The key is to prioritize meditation, as if it were a habit like brushing your teeth or taking a shower. Do it with sincere effort.

Here is what I did to cultivate a relationship with intuition. Try this for at least 21 days.

1. Sit quietly and take long, slow, deep breaths.
2. With every exhale, imagine relaxing your body by sinking into your breath.
3. Inhale for six counts and exhale for six to eight counts. For those who have never meditated before, just do this breathing exercise for a while.

4. Once you feel relaxed, shift your awareness to your heart. Put one hand on your heart and the other on the gut, or two hands on the heart. Choose a position that feels right to you. Take time to connect with your Self.

5. Become aware of how you feel. Ask yourself, "What message do you have for me?" or "What guidance do you have for me today?" Emotionally neutral, open-ended questions are good to start practicing in the beginning. Then wait and continue to relax. Let the answer come to you—whether as a smell, taste, sound, image or simply a knowing feeling. Notice what feelings, thoughts, and bodily sensations arise while you are in this state. It may take several days or weeks to hear or feel the answer. Repetition is your friend.

Over time, it will get easier to discern your intuitive voice.

CHAPTER 4
Déjà vu—one day at a time

"Seeds of faith are always within us; sometimes it takes a crisis to nourish and encourage their growth."

—SUSAN TAYLOR

A few months after his heart failure, Indi was back to his usual, joyful self and was well enough to travel, according to his vet. So, we flew to Houston at the end of December 2013 to visit my sister.

One warm day, Indi was excited to be out for a nice, long walk. Everything seemed fine. But that night, he was breathing faster than normal.

The unusually warm temperatures appeared to put stress on his heart. A vet in Houston advised me to temporarily increase the dosage of Indi's diuretic. Thankfully, 24 hours later, he was back to normal.

Since the weather in Houston stayed relatively warm, perhaps a haircut was in order. Just as I was finishing up his trim, he coughed several times—the same cough I'd heard in Montreal. My heart stopped.

I immediately gave him extra doses of diuretic, as previously instructed, and stayed up all night to monitor his breathing rate. But it wasn't coming down. Indi's breath grew even more labored the next day, so I rushed him to a local vet. The vet immediately put Indi on oxygen. Seeing him struggle for air, I felt hopeless, angry, and guilty that I had let this happen again.

The vet told me that Indi might not make it this time since this was his second heart failure. He added that a lot of dogs die the first time around. But, just like the last time, I knew deep inside that he was going to make it through. Before leaving the hospital, I reassured Indi (or perhaps I was reassuring myself): "You're going to get through this. I just know it."

Back home, my instinct was to call a trusted friend Jessie. She is equal parts acupuncturist, Chinese herbalist and wise soul. After listening to Indi's situation, she said, "You need to talk to Max."

Max, it turned out, was Jessie's client who had special healing gifts and insights. Jessie wasn't aware of his abilities when he first started seeing her, but one day, she experienced it. She had had a lingering concern from many years earlier that she had not shared with anyone. Somehow, Max was aware of it and told her when it would disappear. He can also see energies in the body and discern where the blockages are in certain meridians.

Since then, Max had been sharing his unique knowledge about energy healing, which requires just your hands and mental focus. Jessie felt that Max might be the right person to help Indi.

I called Max. To my amazement, the first thing he told me was, "Indi sacrificed himself in order to help you on your journey to learn about healing and become a better healer."

I couldn't believe what this stranger was saying. How could he know that I was having the very same thoughts? I had never told anyone. It was such a weird and ridiculous idea, even to me. I was afraid if I shared it with anyone, I would be seen as someone who was "way out there." How could Max access my deepest, strangest, innermost thoughts?

I knew instantly that Jessie was right to point me towards Max. He went on to explain the type of energy work that could help Indi right away. Max recommended for me to spend more time with Indi and to perform the healing work that he had just shared.

The conversation with Max deeply challenged me. The whole thing felt far-fetched. Yet, a part of me knew this was the right path, and I had to trust it.

At the hospital that afternoon, I performed this new healing work. As Max had recommended, I held Indi for as long as possible—until the staff told me to leave. For the next two days, I repeated this process three times each day until he was discharged.

Indi survived a second time. The vet increased the dosage of all three of his medications. He told us that with Indi's current condition, he couldn't predict his life expectancy.

"Indi may last a couple of weeks or a couple of months at most," he said. "Manage one day at a time."

As I listened to the vet's prognosis, my heart ached. But a strong voice inside told me not to accept this. Our life together would continue beyond a couple of months. With Indi by my side, I sensed that we were just about to embark on an extraordinary journey.

CHAPTER 5
Repeated patterns

"My life seemed to be a series of events and accidents. Yet when I look back, I see a pattern."

—BENOÎT B. MANDELBROT

I grew up in South Korea. My father was a physics professor, and my mother was a high school science teacher. My family didn't practice a religion or follow any type of spiritual practice. My parents had faith in science. When I was sick, we didn't visit an herbalist or an acupuncturist, like many of my friends did. Instead, my parents took me to the hospital.

In school, I studied hard and got good grades. Upon graduation, I entered a nursing program at a reputable university, on track for a professorship, like my dad.

During those college years, I began to come across weird incidents that couldn't be explained easily with science. The first happened in 1996. As a student nurse attending to patients who had suffered brain damage, there were two octogenarian male patients who had suffered strokes. They were lying on their beds, side by side, unconscious.

Their health charts revealed that both men had been diagnosed with terminal cancer about 10 years earlier. At the time of diagnosis, each of their doctors had indicated that they would have about three months to live.

I reread their charts to make sure I hadn't misunderstood. How was this possible—that two unrelated people, who should have died from cancer 10 years earlier, found themselves lying next to each other at this hospital without any trace of cancer? Strangely, none of my coworkers seemed intrigued. They dismissed this as an odd coincidence.

The second incident happened soon after the first, at the same hospital. A 35-year-old woman was admitted for surgery to remove a brain tumor. The doctors believed it would be a relatively simple procedure. But when I walked into the woman's room, she was howling and screaming, telling the doctors that she didn't want to go through with the operation. They assured her that the tumor would be easy to operate on and that she didn't need to worry. But she was inconsolable: "I don't want to die," she cried. The doctors asked her family members to calm her down.

Watching this scene, I got goosebumps all over my body. I felt the desperation in her voice. She sounded like a person facing certain death.

The next day, apparently the woman had died during the operation. Somehow, she had known she would not survive the surgery. But how?

These events impacted my psyche. They began to open my eyes to a world outside of logic and science.

Then, during my senior year of university, we were required to study an alternative modality and present our findings at the end of the semester. I contacted a local reflexology teacher. She told me she'd become interested in reflexology because the treatments had helped her recover from a chronic kidney disease that had required regular dialysis. When we met at her office, she announced that her kidney function was back to normal.

"Really, just from massaging your feet?", I questioned.

"Yes," she responded, smiling at my disbelief. She must have been used to this kind of reaction. She pulled a book about reflexology theory from her bookcase and gave it to me as a gift.

At home, upon opening the book, I was drawn in by the very first sentence: "The human body is a small universe and is a reflection of the bigger universe."

I ruminated on the sentence for a long time. I didn't quite grasp its significance, but somehow it rang true. Later, I learned that this philosophy is the basis of Traditional Chinese Medicine. It's also a core principle in quantum physics.

After graduating from university in Seoul, I moved to Austin, Texas, to pursue a master's degree in nursing. But after a year, my heart just wasn't into the field of nursing. I felt the limitations of conventional medicine were too great to ignore and thought there must be a better way. As I pondered whether to finish the master's program, I stumbled upon a Chinese medicine school near my home, where visitors could sit in on classes for a week to learn about the program. Their holistic approach was so enjoyable that by the end of the week, I had enrolled in a three-year master's program in Traditional Chinese Medicine (TCM).

For the first time, I was excited about my education. Learning TCM felt right.

During this program, we practiced on volunteer clients. One day, I was treating one of my regular patients, a relatively healthy 30-something female with no history of mental instability. While placing needles on her back to relieve allergy symptoms, she suddenly started talking nonsense (or so I thought):

"I see you. You were a monk in one of your past lives," she said. "I see you praying on top of the mountain, maybe in Tibet, with bare feet. You were so immersed in your prayer and forgot how cold it was. Your feet were frozen."

At first, I thought she was having a hallucination. Then, as suddenly as it began, the episode was over. She started to speak normally again.

I nearly forgot about this until two years later, when I ran across a new modality called BodyTalk.

During one of the sessions as a patient, I complained to the BodyTalk practitioner about my chronic lower back pain. She said the pain was associated with an experience from a past life.

I almost rolled my eyes, thinking, "Oh gosh, am I paying for this kind of nonsense?"

What came out of her mouth next caught me off guard: She said that while I was a monk in Tibet, I had a very severe lower back injury. The memory of that trauma in my cells was still affecting my lower back.

Back then, I didn't believe in past lives. But this was the second person to tell me that I had been a Tibetan monk in a past life. Again, I brushed off these two conversations as coincidences and forgot about them for many years, just like other incidents—until Indi's heart failed.

And there was that gut feeling on the night of Indi's cough and the conversation with Max.

Looking back, there were many inexplicable incidents. I just hadn't found the connection between them yet. With Indi's heart failure, I wondered whether these events were somehow connected. If so, what might that mean for Indi and me?

Then, suddenly, a pattern jumped out at me.

Fractals

Any single incident may look like an isolated event. But by stringing them together, it could reveal a pattern.

In math, fractals are never-ending patterns created by repeating a process over and over.[5] Nature is filled with fractal patterns. The repeated spiral pattern in a seashell is one well-known example of a fractal—so are snowflakes, broccoli, trees, and mountains.[6]

---

5 https://fractalfoundation.org/resources/what-are-fractals/
6 https://webecoist.momtastic.com/2008/09/07/17-amazing-examples-of-fractals-in-nature/

We are surrounded by fractals. And I believe they exist not only in nature but in our lives as well. Random events can have a deeper correlation.

This is most easily discernible in relationships. Often, we attract or are attracted to a similar type of personality repeatedly, sometimes to the detriment of our well-being. You might know someone who complains about their boss at work and then switches their job only to have the same scenario play out again. These patterns continue until we recognize them and then do something to disrupt them.

Many years ago, I helped a Korean woman who was experiencing serious domestic abuse. When she moved to America, her husband refused to let her learn English or to learn how to drive and controlled her every movement. As time went on, it became obvious that her husband was attempting to extort money from her family in exchange for sponsoring her permanent residency.

After a few failed attempts to free her, she finally escaped with the help of the police. She realized that all her life, she had been surrounded by people who were very controlling: her mother, her husband, and so on.

Only when this pattern became apparent was she ready to make a change. She moved away from the abuse and started fresh. Recognizing this pattern saved her life.

In my case, the learning curve was also difficult. I had been raised without the concepts of energy, spirituality or intuition, but now I was encountering incidents that defied explanation. Two 80-something-year-old men who upended doctor's predictions and recovered from terminal cancer diagnoses. A woman who predicted her own death in the operating room. Two different women who told me the same story about my past life. Sensing Indi's heart problem right after his first cough. Max from Dallas…

At first, these events seemed unrelated. But when Indi's heart failed the second time, I had an 'aha moment'. What initially felt like a nudge, became a shove from the universe to get my full attention on phenomena that science can't explain. I was becoming aware of the fractal patterns in my life.

I believed that Indi could live longer than a few months. I could also see that my life path was aligned with an unconventional way of seeing, being, and doing. It was on this path that I might find a way to help Indi—and myself.

As an acorn is coded to become an oak tree (not a palm tree), humans also are born to express themselves with their different tendencies, talents, and potentials. Some are gifted in the arts, some with skills in math, some with the power of care and healing. Recognizing our fractal patterns can help us to express ourselves according to our unique coding. It will help us to grow and better guide us to find our unique path.

When you recognize your fractal, pay special attention to it. It will have an important message for you and that message may change your life.

In my case, these repeated mysterious incidents helped to guide me beyond Traditional Chinese Medicine and towards the broader field of energy medicine, quantum physics, and spirituality. These events were like stepping stones to new perspectives.

When I delved deeper to learn more about energy, it felt like remembering a long-lost memory. This feeling affirmed that I was on the right path.

CHAPTER 6

New city

"Most of us have had regrets and recognize how they can hold us back or keep us stuck in life and relationships. Getting past 'The Past' is important for anyone desiring to live beyond mistakes and the problems they make."

—RON NEFF

When Indi was discharged from the hospital after his second heart failure, he was incredibly weak. He would run out of breath just walking up a set of stairs.

A week after Indi's discharge, we received a phone call from a family in Vancouver. My mother-in-law needed assistance relocating to a nursing home. Without much help from other family members, my husband felt obligated to step up immediately. We had to fly to Vancouver.

With Indi still recovering, I was reluctant to make the trip. But the vet thought it would be okay for my number one patient to fly as long as we took some precautions. We delayed our departure by two weeks, and in the interim,

I consulted with Max. Knowing that Indi would likely be confined to his travel box for 4 hours, he suggested that I envision sending blue light energy to his heart to keep him protected and calm.

The air in the cabin was unusually stuffy, causing Indi to pant constantly.[7]

Thankfully, Indi survived the trip. But his condition continued to decline as we got settled in a new city. He couldn't walk for more than a block without gasping for air.

One day, my husband was leaving our new home in running gear. Since Indi used to go on runs with him, watching him leave without Indi was so agitating that his body suddenly became rigid, and he spontaneously urinated in my arms. Indi had fainted. And I panicked.

I tried reviving him, but he was unresponsive. My heart was pounding as I raced out the door and down the street with Indi in my arms. Fearing that he was dying, I was desperate to find transportation to the local animal hospital.

Thankfully, within the next few minutes, he regained consciousness and his vital signs returned to normal. I was relieved but also realized how dire his situation was. His heart couldn't handle even a little excitement. I immediately regretted coming to Vancouver.

I was now on constant guard and growing anxious with every cough and pant. I blamed myself for:

---

[7] More animal deaths occur on certain airlines. Please do your research before flying with a pet.

- not noticing the early signs of his heart condition
- having previously left him with a friend for an extended backpacking trip
- not taking him to the hospital soon enough
- weakening him by forcing him to endure a long flight

I feared just one more wrong choice could end his life.

Considering the grave situation Indi was in, we needed to find a holistic veterinarian who would think outside the box. Conventional methods could only offer medications to control his symptoms.

Research helped me find Dr. Goldberg from the Vancouver Animal Wellness Hospital. From the very beginning, I felt comforted by his gentle approach. Indi's condition was so severe that Dr. Goldberg was prepared to arrange an appointment with a cardiologist the very next day. We considered it but ultimately decided to wait. The stress of all the tests would be too hard on him.

Instead, over many weeks, we maintained a homemade whole-food diet with natural supplements and served him prescribed medications three times per day. He also received regular home treatments of acupuncture, BodyTalk, and the energy treatment learned from Max. His breathing rate steadied at 24–30 breaths per minute. This was a relief for me.

Given how dependent this little guy was on my decisions, the pressure was mounting.

CHAPTER 7
My emotional compass —Indi's belly

"Beliefs, and the feelings that we have about them, are the language that 'speaks' to the quantum stuff that makes our reality."

—GREGG BRADEN

During our first six months in Vancouver, despite all my efforts, Indi's progress was minimal. His breathing remained labored. We stayed mostly at home, as he was too weak to tackle more than a few blocks. Without air conditioning, the summer heat was extremely hard for him. Heart conditions make the body less adaptable and increase the risk of heatstroke. I often found Indi panting on the floor struggling to stay cool.

During this time, we were caring for my mother-in-law, who was in and out of the hospital while waiting for a place in a nursing home. She didn't trust non-family members to care for her, which put more pressure on the situation.

In the middle of summer, she suffered a major stroke that

left her bedridden. We decided to stay in Vancouver to provide her with care and comfort. We were now committed to Vancouver, though my heart was still in Montreal.

As time passed, these circumstances created friction between my husband and me. In the early days in Vancouver, our relationship had already become strained due to several unpleasant incidents arising from others questioning our interracial relationship.

During this period of tension, Indi's belly looked swollen. The first thought was that maybe he was gaining weight since his activity had diminished dramatically. But it wasn't excess weight. It was water. According to Dr. Goldberg, Indi had developed ascites—water accumulation in his abdomen.

Previously, Indi had experienced failure in the left side of his heart. This resulted in fluid collecting in his lungs, which led to breathing difficulties. When the right side of the heart began to fail, fluid accumulated in the abdomen. This required an increase in Indi's dosage of diuretics. I was upset and disappointed by this news.

Looking into Indi's deep, soulful brown eyes, something was gripping me inside.

> *He is only seven years old, damn it. I need to be strong for the two of us. This little love sponge doesn't deserve to die a premature death.*

He looked as if he was not going to accept it either. After exhausting the treat bowl, he was eager to leave the vet's office.

From that day forward, Indi's belly was measured each morning to monitor the ascites. Over the next three months, there seemed to be a strange correlation between his ascites and the stress level in our household. If either my husband or I was under stress, or if we had an argument, Indi's belly size was measurably larger the next morning. And once the two-legged "noise" returned to normal, so would his belly.

In the later stages of his illness, this became even more obvious. Whenever we were under emotional stress, it seemed to build up in his belly, sometimes within hours. Indi's girth became an instant 'stress-o-meter'. With this little Buddha belly staring us in the face, we could no longer let things bottle up.

The impact of emotions

The impact of emotions on our health has been known for thousands of years. In the Bible, Proverbs 17:22–23 says, "A joyful heart is good medicine, but a crushed spirit dries up the bones." In TCM, emotional imbalance is considered a major cause of disease.

According to quantum physics, everything in this universe—including our thoughts, feelings, and emotions—is composed of energy. Although the energy frequencies of thoughts and emotions are invisible to us, they constantly communicate, interact and influence everything around them. This means that how we feel and what we think can directly impact our physical reality, including the animals in our midst.

Sadly, the impact of our family's emotions seemed to undermine all the other forms of caretaking, such as giving Indi herbs, medicines, and treatments. In his quiet way, he was absorbing our tension.

We experience spillover effects from other people's emotions every day. Have you ever noticed a mood change after spending time with someone who sees the world as 'half glass empty'? Most of us would rather spend our time with happier souls. It just feels better. But the knock-on effect is real in both cases.

If your animals are relatively healthy, the impact of emotions may not be obvious. But, as most would not like to expose their children to family tension, we need to be mindful that animals can also be impacted. And sick animals can be even more sensitive to our thoughts, feelings, and emotions, as we saw with Indi.

Further problems arise when we suppress our emotions. Emotion is energy. They are a natural but temporary state that need to move through us—think how crying helps usher sadness out of the body. Unfortunately, expressing emotions is discouraged in our society, and many of us learn to suppress them early in life. We may bury them somewhere in the body, but over time they accumulate. This can interfere with our physical and mental well-being. A way to move emotional energy is to allow them to be felt and find a way to express them.

It might help to think of emotions as an internal GPS; an indicator that the mind is out of sync with the situation or when our deepest inner desires are being denied. They provide feedback on how we are doing and whether we are on the right path or with the right people.

When we suppress our emotions for a long time, chances are we've grown accustomed to feeling unfulfilled and unhappy. We want to feel good but can't. This is because we are habitual beings and tend to resist change.

If that is what you're facing, try the "stop technique." At the beginning of my journey with Indi, I was plagued by negative thoughts. The "stop technique" helped me escape it. This following method is taught by one of my favorite teachers, Jean Houston. I've also added some of my own flavors.

'Stop' technique

1. Start by thinking of something that brings you joy or a feeling of love. It could be a significant other, your favorite food, or a place. I picture Indi running through the forest with his infectious joy and enthusiasm. That image makes me smile to this day.

2. Now breathe—in through your nose, out through your mouth. As you breathe in, imagine that feeling of joy and love entering your body and mind. As you breathe out, imagine yourself blowing out those negative thoughts and emotions. Practice several times per day until you get used to it. Inhale the good and exhale the bad.

3. When you find yourself in a negative thinking pattern, tell yourself to stop, firmly and loudly. When alone,

I say "stop" out loud and clap my hands at the same time. It instantly breaks the negative state. Then go back to number one: think of something that brings you joy. Breathe that good feeling in through your nose, then blow the negative feelings out through your mouth. Do this until your mood changes.

Practice every day for at least 21 days; more often early on, then less frequently as you take control over those negative thoughts. Similar to building muscle mass in the body, it will take some time to build feel-good muscle.

What helps you to deal with unpleasant situations?

Seeing conflicts as opportunities for growth.

In retrospect, despite how unpleasant this period was for me, the "bad and unfair" experiences in my life have helped me more than the good ones.

Many of us associate conflict with negativity and try to avoid it if we can. If you prefer peace, like me, you may have a tendency to go along with other peoples' ideas rather than speak up and express yourself. But this doesn't make conflict go away. Rather, this tendency often leads to greater inner conflict.

Conflicts and setbacks can be blessings in disguise. They introduce us to our real selves and present opportunities to become greater selves. Often, conflicts can reveal fear-, guilt-, and shame-based beliefs (and others) that keep us captive to unhappiness. When we're willing to see conflict as an opportunity to learn, it can be a real turning point for our growth.

For example, during our first several months in Vancouver, I was busy trying to meet the expectations of others. And, of course, I had my own unspoken expectations of them. It was a vicious cycle. This was the source of my conflict. Only when this realization hit me was I able to grow from it by prioritizing myself. (Further information can be found in "Conscious self-care" at the end of the book.)

Our beliefs shape our perceptions. They influence every action and reaction. Being open to examining our beliefs, (re)actions, and how we perceive conflicts are keys to resolving them. The answers to all our conflicts lie within each of us.

CHAPTER 8
Connecting the dots

"We are like Islands in the sea, separate on the surface but connected in the deep."

—WILLIAM JAMES

Have you ever felt like you're missing something? You look around for an answer, but none is to be found. For a few years, I sensed a deep void inside that nothing could fill. I was constantly questioning my thoughts and convictions. It was like straddling a gap between what my body sensed and what I was able to express. I wondered if this is how animals feel.

While adjusting to life in Vancouver, I continued to seek answers for Indi and a clearer direction for myself. As if the universe heard my pleas, a complimentary free lecture by Jean Houston landed in my inbox. I knew I had to learn more.

Jean is an outstanding teacher with tremendous knowledge of history, culture, quantum science, psychology, anthropology, mythology, and spirituality. She has also worked with many international agencies, including the United Nations. A big part of her teaching is about understanding how our universe works. According to quantum physics, the universe is 99.99 percent energy, which includes all organisms and all matter. We are all connected through the invisible web of energy.

Jean emphasizes the importance of fulfilling one's potential because she understands that each individual's fulfillment could contribute to the larger world through this interconnectivity. The changes we make as individuals—our thoughts, emotions and intentions—influence the whole universe. This philosophy is also reflected in many diverse spiritual practices over thousands of years.

When Jean was young, Albert Einstein, a master of quantum physics, was a guest speaker in her classroom. One kid in the class asked: "How do I become smart like you, sir?" He responded, "Read more fairy tales."

Einstein knew the importance of human imagination and its significant role in helping us reach our potential.

To this day, Jean continues to encourage exploring our intuition and imagination to help us understand the world at large and to reach our goals, whether healing, problem solving, or reinventing ourselves.

Jean's every word was a breath of fresh air. After many long hours listening to her teachings, I realized the missing link was being able to tap into the realms of intuition and imagination. These helped me to begin to see the more refined dots in the tapestry of life.

The more I delved into this knowledge, the more certain I was that Indi and I were meant to share this experience together.

CHAPTER 9
Doing versus being

"We have a tendency to think in terms of doing and not in terms of being. We think that when we are not doing anything, we are wasting our time. But that is not true. Our time is first of all for us to be. To be what? To be alive, to be peaceful, to be joyful, to be loving. And that is what the world needs most. We all need to train ourselves in our way of being, and that is the ground for all action. Our quality of being determines our quality of doing."

—THÍCH NHẤT HẠNH

For the next several months, the focus was on learning more about energy and different types of healing. And although I did everything within my power, Indi's progress wasn't obvious. His breathing was still shallow and slightly elevated, ranging from 24–28 breaths per minute. This lack of progress was disappointing.

Then, one day, the light went on: Because I was constantly fearing that Indi's heart might fail at any moment, I was unconsciously projecting a negative outcome for him. I was not practicing what I had learned—that our thoughts and emotions influence the world around us.

Unbeknownst to me, Indi was likely suffering in my healing hands because of my toxic emotional state.

With Indi, I needed to align my state of being with the mission to help him. A change was necessary. I became more mindful of my thoughts and feelings. When habitual worries came up, I'd use the "stop" technique.

Initially, it was a struggle. My mind kept gravitating towards old negative patterns. But Indi deserved better, so I fought to steer my thoughts towards visualizations of happy outcomes. I called upon my mantra daily.

We are 99.99% energy. Therefore, our energetic state is more powerful than what we do. If we want to emit healthy energy frequencies, then we must be present with ourselves every day, just like cleaning a house.

Slowly, my mood improved, spending less time stewing in the worst-case scenario and appreciating more that Indi was still with me.

This became a regular practice in Indi's treatments. More time was spent on my state of being than pressuring myself to give Indi more treatments. I took extra time to prepare myself before giving a session.

One particular day, the BodyTalk session flowed more easily than usual. I remember experiencing a sense of expansion and lightness like I was floating. With my left hand on Indi's heart, I suddenly felt a click on my fingertips. Until that moment, Indi's breathing had been labored. But, almost instantly, his breathing calmed. Now, I could barely see his ribcage moving. There was no sign of struggle.

Even my husband remarked on this improvement.

This event indicated I was on the right path. From that day forward, instead of doing more to help Indi, I focused more on being at ease and present with my feelings. This was a step towards aligning my energy with my actions.

To my amazement, Indi's breathing remained calm, ranging between 16 to 18 breaths per minute… for the rest of his life.

Most of us are busy doing things. We organize ourselves around 'to do' lists. Yet, fewer are mindful of their energetic state while performing those tasks. For example, consider a person that has high career ambitions. Even by putting in more hours than anyone else, their hard work could still be undermined if they constantly doubt their abilities. Since their effort and energetic state (thoughts and emotions) are not aligned, this subtle energy dissonance can be transmitted and influence those around them.

Whether it is your own health issue, that of your pet, or a loved one, the best thing is to align your *being* with your *doing*. The power of being always overrides the power of doing.

CHAPTER 10

Indi's "voice"

"I shall not commit the fashionable stupidity of regarding everything I cannot explain as a fraud."

—CARL JUNG

Indi's condition was improving significantly. He was breathing more easily, and we were able to go out for short walks.

In August 2015, a good friend, Tamara, invited me to a seminar. However, after learning the speaker wasn't who I expected, I considered canceling. But then something inside nudged me to go.

The seminar was being conducted by Dr. Robert O'Dwyer. His story was that he had become severely sick and had a near-death experience. While recovering, he explored a number of modalities outside his conventional medical training. This seminar was about one of the healing modalities he had learned.

We arrived early and had the opportunity to review a few alternative healing books on display. The first one I picked up was *"Regeneration Healing: The Handbook,"* authored by Ken Graydon, a lifelong healer based in Australia who had compiled more than 60 years of knowledge into his book. Randomly opening the book to page 178, the subject was: "Regeneration of a tooth (or teeth)."

I had to buy the book. A few weeks earlier, Indi had broken a tooth while chewing on raw bone marrow, and the tooth next to it had also become loose. Since he was being fed homemade soft foods, his teeth required regular cleaning, which he disliked. The vet didn't think it was a good idea to clean his teeth professionally or even to remove the loose tooth because of his heart condition. Anesthesia would be too much for his heart. Unfortunately, there was no solution for his broken or loose teeth.

On this journey with Indi, I had learned that coincidences may not be as they appear. Happenings that I'd otherwise consider coincidental would lead to more synchronous events that delivered just the right next step.

To me, it was no coincidence that the book opened up to a chapter about a tooth.

This book was very different from other healing books. It was filled with practical processes and felt alive.

One day, while applying one of the processes for Indi, a pinkish-purple sheen appeared to emanate from the pages. I was astounded. I wiped my eyes, then double-checked with my husband.

He confirmed that this was no hallucination.

The purple sheen became brighter and more obvious as I read. Apparently, other book owners had reported similar experiences. Since purple is the color of healing, it did not seem coincidental. Encouraged by this, I continued the process for Indi every day for a few months.

For more than 18 months, Indi managed without significant setbacks. Dr. Goldberg was impressed with his progress. During one checkup, he told me that when he first saw Indi, he didn't think Indi would survive this long. He said to keep doing whatever I was doing.

Dr. Goldberg's words were encouraging, but I remained concerned about the ascites. I managed it with natural herbs, like dandelion extract and a Chinese herb formula called Wu Ling San, which were gentler on his frail body than a high dose of the prescribed diuretics[8].

One night, after completing one of the processes from *Regeneration Healing*, an idea came to me. Since this book seemed to be generating good results, why not contact the author, Ken Graydon? He had provided an email address in his book.

Ken responded almost immediately. For Indi, he thought the best course of action would be working with an animal communicator named Christina Burki. He had worked

---

8   Disclaimer: I am not a doctor or a vet. I am providing this information for educational purposes only. The contents of this book are not intended to be a substitute for professional medical advice, diagnosis, or treatment. Always seek the advice of your vet or another qualified healthcare provider for any questions you have regarding a medical condition, and before undertaking any diet or other health-related program.

with Christina in the past and was impressed with her work.

Many may have doubts when they hear the term "animal communicator." I had tried animal communication once before in Texas. It had been a disappointment, so I was doubtful when Ken recommended her. But, through Christina's website, I found out she is also a psychotherapist—a credible professional—which gave me comfort.

Indi was a little dude with few barks—not much of a communicator to begin with, at least not in that sense. He only barked when he saw squirrels. Sometimes, he made a whimpering sound when he needed something badly. One day, I returned from work to find him quivering at the door. Something was urgent. Upon exiting the house, he had explosive diarrhea. How long had he been waiting for me to come home? This little guy's patience was admirable.

However, Indi's lack of vocal expression made me wonder whether he was happy. When Ken recommended contacting Christina, I thought that, at the very least, Indi might communicate whether his treatments were helpful for him. It turned out to be one of the best decisions ever made for Indi—or for myself, for that matter.

We connected by email at first. Christina wrote that she would communicate with Indi through a remote session and share what she learned over Skype afterward. I sent her some questions to ask Indi. One was whether my previous extended absences had impacted him (divorce and a backpacking trip).

People around me always said, "Oh, he's just a dog, he wouldn't know the difference." Or, "He probably won't remember." But I always had a feeling that Indi was bothered then, and perhaps might even still be mal-affected.

Christina's first communication was surprisingly accurate, capturing details which hadn't been shared with her.

For example, Christina knew nothing about a change in Indi's behavior after my marital breakup. Indi was used to sleeping in the bedroom, next to his humans. But after the divorce, my ex-husband made him sleep in the living room because his new girlfriend was allergic to dogs. During this time, Indi soiled the carpets and altogether behaved badly. After we were reunited, though, he never had another accident.

Also, in my email communication with Christina, I didn't mention that my life completely changed as a result of Indi's illness. But, as you'll read in Christina's first communication with Indi, he could see the change in me which he shared with her. Because of this, I instantly knew the message was from Indi, not from Christina.

The first communication with Indi, October 22, 2015

I (Christina) first asked for permission to communicate with him (Indi).

Indi: " I have been waiting for you the whole time since I already felt that there would be a communication between us." (I have been feeling him the whole morning already.)

I told him that he is very sensitive.

Indi: "Oh yes I am!"

I told him how beautiful he is and that he has such a wonderful gentle soul.

Indi: "Thank you!"

I asked him how he feels.

Indi: "Not all good and not too bad."

What do you feel in your body?

Indi: "Sometimes a sharp pain by my heart and sometimes pain in my stomach. I feel at the same time good in myself. I am happy and love to live!"

That is very good.

I heard about your history, about Jasmine and her ex-husband, and that they split up. How was that for you?

Indi: "Bad. I didn't want to leave anyone, and Jasmine went away. I missed her and had to stay where he wanted me to stay. I felt lonely and not in balance and was sad. I can imagine that I was not that gentle dog anymore. I felt lost."

How was it for you when you were brought back to Jasmine?

Indi: "Good Heaven on Earth! I was so thankful to see her again!!"

How about the five-month world trip?

How was this for you to stay behind?

Indi: "Bad. I didn't like it at all. I missed them so much, although that friend was ok. I felt like I had been betrayed. I was very, very sad deep inside of me!"

Everyone and everything can feel trauma. I will work with this later in the session.

Indi: "It was really bad and I felt sick a lot inside and had the feeling that they wouldn't come back!"

How was it when they came back?

Indi: "It was great and at the same time I started to feel distrust. I didn't know when and if they would leave me again."

Are you still afraid of missing them again?

Indi: "Oh yes I am."

I can imagine that they haven't been away since those times, could you imagine letting go of that fear?

Indi: "More or less but it is still there!"

Where in your body do you feel your fear?

Indi: "In my heart. I love Jasmine very much she is wonderful, and I couldn't imagine missing her again!"

You got sick in your heart. Do you have a lot of fear or is there anything else that bothers you?

Indi: "I have sorrows about Jasmine. She is wonderful and I feel that she has too much stress sometimes. It is a busy life and I wouldn't love to miss her. She feels sometimes so tired, and I love her but can't do a lot for her."

"Jasmine should be more aware of herself and me. I feel that when I am sick, she is more with me and she cares more for me and herself. My sickness makes her more aware of herself and we share more time with each other."

She loves you too, a lot.

Indi: "Yes I know that!"

What do you think about letting go of the fearful thought in your heart and Jasmine will take more care of you and herself? Could you imagine letting go of fear?

Indi: "Yes!"

> *Can I help you?*
>
> *Indi: "Yes."*
>
> *Jasmine, Indi wants me to tell you that he never wants to be left alone for so long again. He needs you to be with him!*
>
> *He has this message for you:*
>
> *Indi: "Jasmine, I love you with all of my heart and I missed you so much in the past. You are so full of love but sometimes you have too much to do. I am scared for you. I don't want to miss you again because you mean the world to me. Please promise me that you will take better care of yourself and take more time for us, I feel then that I can let go of my fear! I love you. Your Indi"*

This communication confirmed that Indi was very much aware of what was going on. What struck me the most was that I was his whole world, but he was only one part of mine. I also had a husband, family, friends, and my job. For Indi, my absence must have been like losing everything, all at once.

I began to understand Indi's emotional state and how he might have felt—a mixture of deep sadness and fear of abandonment.

Indi's encouragement to take better care of myself amazed me as well. I thought I was caring for myself, but obviously not well enough. Reading Indi's message, he seemed to know what I needed better than I did.

After giving Indi a voice through Christina, things shifted almost immediately. To my surprise, the day after the communication, Indi's belly shrank noticeably. He even seemed to have more energy—that day, he walked to the nearby pet store three times and didn't want to come home. On one of those visits, the rascal even tried escaping with a dried chicken breast without paying. Seeing him so energetic and happy, it lightened my heart. Indi appeared to have freed himself from the worry of being abandoned again.

Coincidences?

Many believe that our life is a sum of random events.

Carl Jung wrote about synchronicity as a "meaningful coincidence," or the coming together of seemingly unrelated and improbable events.

Science itself is built on coincidences—finding the pattern in supposedly random phenomena. When something happens once, no one notices. But only when it happens a second, third, or fourth time, do people pay attention.

What if there is an invisible thread weaving through every event in our lives? Maybe there is a deep order in what seem to be random coincidences, but we haven't discovered it yet.

In a universe where most things are dead, and we are the most advanced living species, it is hard to find meaning in coincidences. But it could be possible that our world is actually a living, conscious being—a gigantic, living organism. Wouldn't this perspective change everything?

In his book, *The Living Universe*, Duane Elgin lays out growing scientific evidence to support this perspective: that the universe is a living entity that constantly evolves. The body, also a living entity, doesn't do things randomly. Every action within our body has purpose. Similarly, it is not far-fetched to think that every action in the universe follows a deep and meaningful order.

Therefore, coincidences could just be purposeful communications from a living universe. They can open our minds to new perspectives on long-held beliefs.

Jung believed that seeing the interconnectedness in life is a foundation of spiritual awakening. Through synchronicity, we can access life's deeper meanings.

> ### How do animal communicators work?
>
> "The word *animal* comes from the Latin, anima, which means life principle, breath, air, soul, and living being. Recognizing the spiritual essence of animals and respecting them as fellow intelligent beings is vital to facilitate interspecies telepathic exchange. Telepathic communication involves the direct transmission of feelings, intentions, thoughts, mental images, emotions, sensations and pure knowing. Animals are able to communicate with humans who are open to the telepathic connection. They get your intentions, emotions, images, or thoughts behind the words."[9]
>
> Through a telepathic connection, animal communicators can tune into an animal's specific energy frequency, similar to dialing into a particular radio station. Here's a real world example:

---

9 https://www.animaltalk.net/AboutAnimalCommunication/

In the late '90's, Cristina Zanato began scuba diving in the Bahamas. Early on in her diving, she repeatedly was approached by a shark with a fishhook embedded inside its mouth. Although uncertain of its intentions, she eventually gathered the courage to stick her hand into the shark's mouth to remove it. The shark somehow knew that her gesture was not going to be harmful.

Upon further dives, she was surprised when this same shark began to nuzzle her and seek her affection. Soon after, more hook-laden sharks started showing up. To this day, she has removed over 300 hooks. Through her love and calm demeanor, she was able to channel thoughts telepathically with this apex predator.

As in any profession, not all animal communicators are alike. Nor do they all offer quality services. Before meeting Christina, I had an experience with another animal communicator. She claimed to be an expert but seemed to care more about her time and money than the animals. She had a few celebrity clients. But a good marketer doesn't necessarily make a good practitioner.

If you are interested, try out a few animal communicators and see whether they are a good fit for you and your animals. Getting a recommendation from people you trust is always a good option.

CHAPTER 11
Three times, not a charm

"The idea that some lives matter less is the root of all that is wrong with the world."
—PAUL FARMER

Before Christina, Indi had slowed down quite a bit because of his ascites, and walking had become an infrequent activity for him. But since the communication with Christina, he had newfound energy and developed a naughty new habit. When we went out for our daily walks, he'd tug me in the direction of Bosley's, the neighborhood pet store, just around the corner from our home.

Outside their store, they offered two fresh bowls of water. Indi wouldn't enter Bosley's until he had his fill. This was his "happy hour." But inside there were treats and toys to explore.

With his sweet gentle nature, he quickly established himself as royalty at Bosley's. The store attendants greeted him by name with treats in hand. Before contact with Christina, going to the pet store had been an occasional activity, but it now became routine: morning, afternoon, and evening. If he didn't visit his favorite pet store, his walks were never completed. Sometimes, he insisted on going to the store at 7 am, well before it was even open. Ever the persistent fellow, we would queue up together in front of the store, like it was a Black Friday sale at Best Buy, until he was convinced nobody was there.

When open, Indi would steer himself behind the cashier's desk. The store manager, Jessica, had developed a particular bond with Indi and would give him a massage in idle moments. Indi loved her touch so much that sometimes he couldn't be coaxed to leave. If there were other furry critters getting their treats, Indi quietly waited until they left, keeping his distance. He wanted alone time with the staff for his treats and massage. It was quite entertaining to watch his character come alive in the store. He was quiet and patient—but stubborn.

I wondered why he liked to go to the store so much. In a subsequent communication, Christina revealed that the store had a special loving and healing energy.

Around Christmas 2015, Indi's bowel movements changed. In the past, he sometimes experienced runny stools for a day or two, but quickly recovered. It was likely that his enlarged liver and ascites were inhibiting normal digestive function. But this time around, his symptoms lasted longer.

When they didn't go away, although concerned, I didn't feel it was yet serious enough to take him to a hospital. He still had energy and was drinking and eating well.

On December 29th, about five days or so after these symptoms started, Indi came to bed right after his nighttime ritual. He and I had already settled in to sleep when my husband walked into the bedroom and blurted, "Indi's bleeding!"

"What do you mean?" I asked.

"There's fresh blood in his stool. We need to take him to the hospital." He explained.

"Oh, but he seems okay now. We can take him to the vet tomorrow." I responded.

With urgency in his voice, he said, "No, it's serious. We have to go now."

I had my doubts, but we took Indi to the hospital. It was 10:30 pm. In the waiting room, there were three other dogs, all lying quietly next to their owners. Indi became quite inquisitive, walking all around to investigate the other patients and the hospital. He seemed to be the only one with any life and energy. *Should he even be here?*

When it was our turn, the vet listened to Indi's health history and our current concern.

The vet then examined him. After two years of living with congestive heart failure (CHF), Indi's body showed the obvious signs of advanced CHF: an enlarged heart and liver and ascites.

With an X-ray in hand, the vet showed us how advanced Indi's condition had become. Indi's heart and liver were three times larger than those of a "normal" dog. His heart occupied almost all the space in his chest cavity. "I have never seen such a big heart in my life," the vet said. "Given his condition, you may want to consider putting him down."

"What?" I couldn't believe what she was saying.

I'm not against euthanasia when suffering is great. But Indi was still vibrant, breathing calmly, and showed no outward signs of distress except that he had diarrhea with a little bit of blood. He was still eating and drinking well and, most importantly, his eyes were bright like stars. I could tell that his spirit was still very strong.

"We can try to help him, but with his condition there is a high chance he may not make it," the vet continued.

At this point, I was very uneasy with this vet's approach. She was recommending euthanasia based solely on the X-ray and was completely disregarding Indi's current vibrant state. You can't measure a life in numbers and tests alone.

I was quite upset at this point and told the vet, "I'd like to take Indi home."

The vet immediately responded, "Indi has a better chance at the hospital than at home. At least we can hydrate him through IV."

I was about to say, "I don't think so," but then my husband interjected.

"I think we should consider her recommendation. Let's leave Indi at the hospital at least for a day. He is probably dehydrated from diarrhea. At least he can get some hydration through an IV," he said, looking quite concerned. I knew he still felt guilty for not taking Indi to the hospital when his heart had failed the first time. Since then, he'd wanted to do everything medically possible to help Indi.

My husband placed more trust in Western medicine than myself. My view is that Western medicine is a necessary tool at times but overusing it can cause more harm than good, especially for weak and delicate patients like Indi.

I wasn't happy with the idea of leaving Indi behind with this vet. I had an uncomfortable, nagging feeling, even though Indi's situation didn't seem as dire as it had the previous two times. But, in the end, I relented. While my husband signed the admission papers, I held Indi and whispered to him not to be afraid. We would come get him soon. We left Indi at the hospital around 3:30 am.

The next day, before heading to the hospital, I emailed Christina. She was on vacation in Bali with her family for the New Year but was quite concerned about Indi. She was even kind enough to offer a communication on New Year's Eve.

Upon arrival at the hospital the next morning, Indi was in a small stainless-steel box with an IV drip in his left leg. He looked scared and tired, less vibrant than the night before. I picked him up and held him to my chest. Since he had been caged overnight, I thought he might want to walk around a bit. But he didn't want to move.

This just didn't feel right. "Why does he look weaker than last night?" I wondered.

Then a different vet came to talk to me. She said Indi was doing fine. He was stable but hadn't eaten anything yet. She told me they had started him on antibiotics.

"What? Why?" I asked. There had been no mention of antibiotics the night before with the other vet. Indi was to be hydrated, nothing more.

She suspected Indi's intestines were inflamed and bleeding as a result of frequent diarrhea. The antibiotics would prevent infection. As well, she would like to monitor him for a little longer.

I stayed with Indi and held him for another 40 minutes. There was no sign of movement; he stayed glued to my chest. He was no longer the curious investigator who had been walking all over the hospital just 12 hours earlier. I felt like he was telling me, "Mommy, I don't feel good here. Please take me home."

However, the vet wanted to see Indi eat before letting him go home. According to her, Indi was doing well. But I felt conflicted.

Stepping outside for a brief walk to get some air, I was torn between the vet's opinion and my instinct to take him home. Christina hadn't contacted me yet. But how I wished I could talk to Indi directly.

Then I remembered Max from Dallas. We had communicated a few times in the past, and he had always given helpful suggestions. He, like Christina, could sense things from a distance, so I texted him about Indi's situation and waited. But an hour later, there was still no message from either of them.

I went back inside the hospital to see a wagging tail. However, in holding him, it felt like he had weakened further. His legs were hanging between my arms without any sign of strength. It was as if his life force was diminishing contrary to the vet's assessment. The vet thought it was still too soon to take him home.

Undecided, I left the hospital and sat on a bench to meditate. That's when I received an email from Christina. She had connected with Indi. She relayed that he wanted to come home. His time in the hospital was bringing him closer to the end. He really wanted to be home.

My heart sank. This is what I had felt as I held Indi at the hospital. He had been trying to communicate that he wasn't doing well.

Around the same time, Max also responded, confirming that Indi would be better at home with me.

I kicked myself again. Each time I didn't listen to my intuition, Indi paid the price. This time, facing a medical professional's opinion, I hadn't had the courage to act.

I called the hospital immediately.

We picked up Indi 16 hours after his admission. The staff told us Indi had just eaten and they gave us medications, including antibiotics.

He couldn't leave the hospital fast enough, his tail wagging furiously. But when he got home, he literally collapsed on the bed, and subsequently, he relieved himself on the bedsheets. This had never happened before. He was so weak he couldn't even control his bowels. For the first time in a very long time, I was scared for Indi. I had never seen him so weak and fragile. He barely moved from that spot for the next 48 hours. Spending the New Year's in bed together, I promised him that I would find the courage to trust my intuition.

How do I know whether I am making the right decision for my pet?

For those facing a similar dilemma, there is no right or wrong decision. Looking back at all the decisions I made regarding Indi—even if they were considered mistakes at the time—they were like stepping stones that helped me learn how and when to trust my intuition. Like learning to walk, falling is a part of the learning process. Each mistake and regret were my stepping stones. Because of them, I learned how my intuition communicates—through feelings, bodily sensations, and so on.

If faced with the same situation today, I would be able to make a quicker decision only because of my past experiences. Whatever decision you might make with a beloved pet, if it comes from the heart, it will be the best one for that given moment. Once decided, do your best to take the appropriate actions.

Most importantly, keep an open mind and ask yourself: What can I learn from this situation to better trust myself?

CHAPTER 12
Seeds of inspiration

"Miracles are not contrary to nature but only contrary to what we know about nature."
—ST. AUGUSTINE

Over the next two days, Indi was completely in my care.

Although this ordeal had weakened him, I didn't want to give him antibiotics, suspecting that they would do more harm than good. Instead, to give his inflamed gut time to heal, my instinct was to put Indi on a 40 hour fast. Considering his condition, this made me nervous, but trusted that it was the right thing to do. He was sleeping nonstop and showing no sign of hunger. However, in order to prevent dehydration, I periodically awakened him to provide water and a little bit of coconut water for electrolytes.

For the next 10 days, I canceled all activities and appointments. If these were Indi's last days on this planet, I wanted to spend them with him, uninterrupted. We were glued together in bed. During this time, I visualized green energy—another known healing color associated with the heart chakra—emanating from my heart and hands.

To end his fast, at Max's suggestion, I gave Indi goat milk. Unlike cow's milk, raw goat milk reduces inflammation. It's soothing to the gut.

At first, I fed him just 2 tablespoons of goat milk to make sure he could keep it down. After several hours and no sign of ill effects, his big brown eyes pled for more. He instinctively knew that goat milk was good for him and finished every drop. Finally, a win for the home team.

Two and a half days after his discharge from the hospital, Indi ate a small amount of his regular food: home-cooked pumpkin with a little bit of chicken. Pumpkin also fights inflammation. Back when he had minor digestive issues, cooked squash or pumpkin with cooked chicken alleviated them.

Indi handled the food well. He not only finished it but kept it all down. His bowel movements improved as well. Encouraged by his progress, I started to feed him small amounts of food every few hours.

Five days after his emergency visit, I woke up to find Indi in front of his food bowl. Obviously, he was a hungry little man, and instead of waking me, he sat quietly waiting for me to get up. The sparkle had returned to his eyes, and they clearly said, "I am starving. I would like some food. Please." I nearly cried.

He finished the bowl. I was relieved to watch him eagerly gobble down a second one.

For the next five days, Indi ate voraciously. His improving health allowed for resumed daily visits to his favorite pet store. The staff had noticed Indi's absence and welcomed him back with extra treats and love. They were impressed with his comeback story. The manager at the store commented on how strong and vibrant Indi looked after his ordeal. His body showed obvious signs of illness: a swollen tummy and enlarged liver were noticeable. But he wasn't slowing down. His spirit shone through his eyes even stronger than before the hospitalization.

About four weeks after his misadventure, I was inspired to take him to his favorite forest, in downtown Vancouver: Stanley Park. We had expected to carry him around, but, to our amazement, Indi burst out of the car with unbounded energy. He was full of pure joy and excitement, running around like a puppy.

It was unbelievable! This was the little fellow for whom the vet had recommended euthanasia just four weeks earlier. He was full of life that day and for many more after that.

Was it a miracle? The Merriam-Webster dictionary defines a miracle as "an extremely outstanding or unusual event, thing, or accomplishment." The Latin root word for miracle, *mirari,* means "to wonder or awe." The curiosity that arises from this wonder or awe often leads to discovery and wisdom. We tend to dismiss things that are beyond our belief systems, but miracles are more common than we are led to believe.

In *The Extraordinary Healing Power of Ordinary Things*, Dr. Larry Dossey writes candidly about how medical professionals are taught to ignore miraculous healings. He also says it is common practice in medical journals to dismiss miraculous healings as "outliers." According to Sir William Osler, who is considered the father of modern medicine, "Phenomenal, even what could be called miraculous cures, are not uncommon."

Another reason we don't hear more about miraculous healings is that many medical professionals, fearing a loss of reputation, hesitate to speak openly about them. But if these miraculous events are not uncommon, they should be studied. Research could expand the field of science and help us to understand how to bring balance back to our body.

Miracle or not, Indi continued to surprise the veterinarians, consistently defying their predictions. It had been nearly two years since the vet in Houston predicted Indi wouldn't live more than a couple of months. The most recent vet at the emergency hospital thought he should already be deceased. Not only was he not on his deathbed, he was living fully. How did I know? By looking into those deep brown eyes and seeing pure joy.

On that day in Stanley Park, Indi's will to live was on display. I was determined to help. And along the way we had met amazing people like Christina and Max, who were now part of Team Indi.

Maybe this is how miracles happen: It starts with one person believing in something and as we move forward, we find allies. When enough of us believe and act on what seems like a remote possibility, amazing things can happen.

Since Indi had almost lost his life twice before, witnessing his miraculous recovery planted the seed for this book. I initially brushed it off as a ridiculous idea since writing was one of my least favorite activities. But it repeatedly emerged during Indi's recovery.

Then Christina told me that Indi had also encouraged this idea. He thought that sharing our journey could inspire others to explore and deepen connections with their own animals.

Sometimes love is the best medicine.

Indi's communication to me relayed from Christina, January 16, 2016

He would still need acupuncture needles for his tension in his hips. When I send healing energy to the liver and heart, I feel that they were in the same frequency, bright and wonderful energy in both organs.

He needs happiness and laughter, and you should start writing your book.

He wants you to tell your thoughts to him and feel what he tells you as an answer.

You should write the book in the form where you take your process as an example. So people realize they can trust their feelings and their animals.

Maybe even ask the vet for confirmation that he thought Indi would have been gone much earlier. Indi said it might be an interesting book for vets as well.

Indi would love to have his and your story in your book!

He wanted a cuddle from me with love and energy and fresh laughter and happiness.

He is so so thankful for everything!

When I send him the hug, I felt this fresh laughter and happiness as well.

Warm thoughts and a cuddle to Indi,

Christina

CHAPTER 13
Nothing is impossible!

*"Dogs are not our whole life,
but they make our lives whole."*

—ROGER A. CARAS

For the next two months, Indi continued to surprise everyone. He was excited to open his eyes every morning and always started and ended his day with a visit to Bosley's. A treat and a massage were always awaiting him. He was a master at finding joy in simple things. Everyone adored him. On the weekends, he particularly enjoyed visits to the park. Strangers often mistook him for a puppy and always commented on how big and bright his eyes were.

Unfortunately, despite all my efforts, Indi's belly continued to accumulate water. His ascites began to slow him down. The water became too heavy for him to carry. His walking slowed and his facial hair started to turn white. In April 2016, Dr. Goldberg, recommended draining the water from his belly by performing an abdominal tap (paracentesis) to make him feel more comfortable.

Dr. Goldberg was aware of our special relationship. He

allowed me to participate in Indi's paracentesis procedure. Christina communicated to Indi that this would happen. She relayed back to me that Indi was okay with it. I held him during the procedure and talked to him the entire time. He was calm and eventually fell asleep in my arms without anesthesia. He came out of the clinic 1.2 liters lighter with a wagging tail. Afterward, he continued with his daily routine as if nothing had happened and nothing could stop him.

Six weeks after his first paracentesis, he needed another one. This time, less water was drained because his liver had become larger and was taking up more space in his abdominal cavity. He had lost so much muscle mass that his enlarged liver and ribs could be felt with my hands. It really hit me when, for the first time, he struggled to climb the stairs onto the bed. The water seemed to be accumulating faster than before.

We both sensed that our time together was coming to an end. But this didn't slow Indi down. Despite his declining health, he expressed many times through Christina that he loved his life. On the days he couldn't walk very far, he simply enjoyed being outside to catch a whiff of the roses. His highlight, of course, was his tri-daily appearances at the local pet shop.

Our connection had become so deep that he didn't want to leave just yet. But he didn't want me to feel guilty when the time came.

Each day, Indi dictated the pace. Some days he was more energetic, while on others, he liked to simply stand watching people. Just spending time together made us both happy.

One day, though, instead of watching him and waiting for him to move on, I decided to mimic him.

As he slowed down, I slowed down. When he stood still, I would sit nearby. I remained relaxed but aware. It felt like time had slowed for both of us, like a scene from *The Matrix*. Even my breathing slowed. I could feel the gentle hug of the wind and the warm touch of the sun. There was a mild scent of sweetness in the air. I understood what Indi enjoyed about standing still. Our eyes met.

"Get it?" he seemed to ask.

"Yeah, I think so," I replied.

It was such a heavenly moment. With his simplicity, Indi showed me how to find joy and appreciate life no matter the circumstances. In his quiet way, he told me that joy is a choice we make at any given moment. It is about opening our eyes and being fully present to recognize the extraordinary qualities in common things. After all, the most important things in life are free and irreplaceable. We tend to forget to appreciate them and, instead, spend too much time chasing material things. But the joy from achievement or possession doesn't last forever.

Our animals remind us how to live in the 'here and now', which is an attribute of a great spiritual being.

After the first paracentesis, the procedure became routine every few months. On a future visit, Dr. Goldberg's associate asked whether he could take a photo of Indi's body. He had never seen a living animal with such a big heart and liver. He was surprised that Indi was still alive with this condition. Not only that, because he was behaving like a healthy dog and asking for more treats, this doctor announced, "Nothing is impossible for Indi!"

As Indi's condition progressed, my days became simpler. I rarely went out except to work and spent most of the time at home with Indi. The things previously required for my happiness, like shopping and socializing, were no longer necessary. As the Dalai Lama once said, the secret to happiness is to "keep it simple." Because of Indi, these words finally resonated.

CHAPTER 14
My transformative guide

"Everything I know I learned from dogs."
–NORA ROBERTS

Vets had been consistently warning that Indi might not make it. The most recent hospitalization, though, felt different from the previous two. Since Indi had escaped death for the third time, every minute became more precious.

I didn't think it was possible that our bond could get any deeper, but it did. Christina played an increasingly important role. She let me know what Indi needed or what he wanted me to know. She often confirmed my thoughts regarding Indi and added valuable suggestions. She became not only a voice for Indi, but also a sounding board for my intuition about him. In turn, because my relationship with my own 'SELF' was deepening, this started to shift things between Indi and me in a very profound way.

Through his eyes, he communicated what he wanted and needed. I could even sense his silent pleas for help from other rooms. Sometimes, I would have a sudden urge to check on him, often finding him stuck awkwardly or sitting on the edge of the bed waiting for a lift to the floor. Along with these incidences, confidence in my intuition grew stronger. Despite his condition, Indi's life essence persisted through his resilience and the strength of his soul every day.

Jean Houston wrote in her book, *Mystical Dogs: Animals as Guides to Our Inner Life*:

> *"Dogs are the great companions of our lives. They teach us, love us, care for us even when we are uncaring, feed our souls, and always, always give us the benefit of the doubt. With natural grace, they give us insight into the nature of the good and often provide us with a mirror of our better nature, as well as a remembrance of once and future possibilities."*

For Houston, dogs are "holy guides to the unseen worlds." She also said that "Animals stretch our boundaries, prompting us to ask great questions again of ourselves and of existence." I couldn't agree more.

Dogs exhibit unconditional love, a quality that characterizes only the most highly evolved beings. When my eyes were finally opened to this, I could see Indi's wisdom more fully. Our bond transformed into a deeper spiritual connection.

I believe that Indi came into my life as a spiritual guide to help me on my journey.

Indi, in his quiet, inspiring way, brought so much awareness into our family. He taught me that deep listening is the key to finding a deeper connection, whether it is with our animals, our body, or our spirit. There is real power in giving a voice to silence.

Because of Indi, I now hear my inner voice and am in tune with my "SELF." Indi was my Duru. That was his purpose. And that's why he chose me, without hesitation, the moment we met.

CHAPTER 15
Bar-hopping!

"Dogs die. But dogs live, too. Right up until they die, they live. They live brave, beautiful lives. They protect their families. And love us. And make our lives a little brighter. And they don't waste time being afraid of tomorrow."

—DAN GEMEINHART

As summer began, we spent more time outdoors, enjoying the warmth after a long rainy season. One day, we were standing in front of our favorite bakery waiting for my husband to come out with goodies. Two men walked towards us. Both of them were really tall and big, like pro-wrestlers. They were wearing leather jackets and projected an air that said, "Don't mess with us."

Indi was sitting in a collision course with these two giants, but he stood his ground and stared straight at them. I was about to move Indi, but then they broke into smiles. This was Indi's superpower, making people smile. If you were not smiling already, he would stare you into submission.

Summer in Vancouver is beautiful. As the days grow longer, everyone spends time outside.

Maybe it was the excitement that summer brings to the city, but despite his condition progressing, Indi added a strange new habit to his daily routine. He started getting up super early, waking me up by scratching at the door. When this happened for the first time, I thought he wanted to go outside to do his business. Instead, he slowly meandered over to the pet store—at five in the morning! When Indi realized he couldn't go inside, he decided to go for a stroll. Oddly, he walked in a direction he had never been before. He headed towards a busy retail shopping street.

He started by sniff-shopping the liquor store, then would move on to each subsequent venue. After an extended walk around the neighborhood, we arrived back at his favorite pet store. At 6 am, I lifted him up to show that nobody was inside to give him a treat or a massage. He finally gave up and sauntered home. This new routine went on through June and July. Unlike Indi, I struggled to adapt to this 5 am walk routine.

Then one night, he wanted to go out after 10 pm. This was, again, unusual for him. After realizing the pet store was closed, he headed to the busier side of our street.

I couldn't understand. The area was filled with bars and restaurants. There should have been nothing of interest for a four-legged 'player.'

I was sure he would turn around as soon as we got there. Instead, he stopped by one bar after another and tried to gain entry to each. Indi was bar hopping! Dressed in my almost-ready-for-bed outfit, I wasn't prepared for the scene. But it didn't matter; Indi looked like he was having a really good time. People loved him, whether or not they'd had too much to drink. Crowds of people came to say hello and adore him.

After spending an hour wandering around the bars, Indi showed no sign of tiredness. In the end, I had to carry him away from this star walk because I was ready for bed. Upon arriving home, it was close to midnight, well past, at least, one of our bedtimes.

This new behavior continued, so we now had early-morning and late-night routines. I sometimes worried that he was overexerting himself. I tried to persuade him not to go to the bars. But he was insistent and wouldn't leave willingly. So I carried him home. I thought this was peculiar behavior for a dog. Why did he want to go to bars night after night? I understood the pet store, but why the bars? I emailed Christina to ask Indi. His answer was brilliant.

This communication between Christina and Indi took place on July 18, 2016.

Below is the copy of Christina's email to me after the communication.

> *Today Indi only needed a short tune in.*
>
> *I asked Indi what he loves about the barhopping.*
>
> *His answer: "To make people happy and to feel their energy. There is a special energy, and I feel good to be there sometimes and to feel them. I love touching people's hearts in the pub."*

I was humbled by the wisdom of this frail 15-pound dog. His mission in life was clear. And, despite his condition, he was living his life's purpose to his final breath. Indi's message challenged the traditional concept of retirement.

In his simple and quiet way, Indi showed me the answer: There is no retiring from life's purpose already embedded in our heart.

The state of Indi's health wasn't an issue for him. Yet, my fear of losing him was holding him back. I needed to find the courage to become bigger than that fear.

From then on, I surrendered to Indi's will. He continued bar hopping and meeting new people until two days before his death.

CHAPTER 16
Beautiful death

"The bond with a true dog is as lasting as the ties of this earth will ever be."

—KONRAD LORENZ

The last Saturday in July was a great day. After his third visit to Bosley's, he signaled it was time to head over to the bar district.

It was a beautiful afternoon. The streets were busy, and the patios were packed with people enjoying drinks. Wearing his muscle shirt, Indi casually approached the first bar, hoping to enter.

As usual, he resisted my pleas that he couldn't go in. He then steered to the next bar and stopped at the entrance, hoping for an entry exception. It went on like this from bar to bar.

As always, everywhere we went he seemed to mesmerize people with his big, soulful brown eyes. "Oh my god, look at this puppy. His eyes are so beautiful." They didn't notice how emaciated he was inside of his shirt.

Indi was on a mission to cover every single bar in the area

that day. After an hour of bar hopping, Indi showed no sign of letting up. But, worried about his heart, I picked him up and headed home.

On our way back, we found a bench in a quiet area where birds were playing in a pool of water. Feeling guilty about shortening his bar-time, we sat for a while and watched the birds play, just the two of us.

I've experienced similar moments in the past, but the peace and beauty in those minutes was indescribable. It was as if we were wrapped in celestial energy. I didn't want it to end. Strangely, my gut was telling me that Indi orchestrated this moment.

What I didn't know was that this amazing outing would be our last. The next day, Indi seemed tired. He usually ate his dinner with us but sometimes he skipped meals when he was tired. So I wasn't worried.

But then, in the middle of our dinner, my instincts perked. He was flat on the ground with one leg caught in his blanket, too weak to get up. I lifted him, but he was too shaky to stand. He seemed to be in shock. There was fear and confusion in his eyes, or maybe it was my own fear and confusion.

I had a nervous sensation in my gut and a chill in my spine. Knowing this time would eventually come, I thought I was prepared for it. But I wasn't.

Over the next 48 hours, I cancelled all appointments and spent the time caressing his back and tummy while whispering how much I loved him. He was very calm. He seemed to be present and was hearing everything. This time, though, I hoped my instincts were wrong and that Indi would once again regain his strength.

The next morning, Indi still looked very weak but did manage to eat some breakfast. That gave me a glimmer of hope, but it faded quickly. By afternoon, it was clear that his desire for food was completely gone and that he had little strength left.

I was now certain that Indi wouldn't get better. These were his final hours, but I didn't want him to go. Tears streamed down my cheeks.

That day, I asked Christina to connect with Indi. When I received the communication between Indi and Christina by email, I hesitated to open it for a few minutes. My heart was already pumping so loud, as if it knew what the email would say.

This was her email on August 1, the day before Indi's death.

From: Christina Burki Date: 08-01-2016 11:57 PM (GMT-08:00)

To: 'Jasmine Hong' Subject: tune in

Dear Jasmine

With tears I write to you.

He is sad and very tired. He feels that his lifetime is up soon. He would love to go on, but his body is telling him that it is soon time to say goodbye.

His spirit will stay with you always!

His body tells him to give up and he looks back and knows he had such a wonderful time, and he loves to be with you, but he feels it is soon time to go.

He feels it is enough.

Despite his bright eyes, that is because his soul still shines through, but his body is now too weak and tired. When I felt him outside, it felt that he is not really here anymore.

When I went into his body the left side was very weak and his heart had problems.

Nearly no energy left.

He doesn't want to take supplements.

He wants you to be there with him and he would love to pass over by himself, when he needs support, he will let you know.

You can send him love and acceptance on his soul level that you let him go.

All of his organs are exhausted and very, very tired.

He didn't want to do any more healing processes.

He wants to be in peace and focus only on peace and feeling good and letting go.

> *I (Indi) have to tell you (Christina) "Jasmine, don't be sad. I will always be with you."*
>
> *Let her stay close with me in the next day or so. I will be always with her and tell her that I love her always. Jasmine can pass on the love I gave her so the world will become a better place.*
>
> *Let her be touched by my love and spread my message and my unconditional love. She (Jasmine) should live her vision NOW. I helped her to be on her path, now it is her turn.*
>
> *I did a deep meditation with Indi. With angels and two animals that are my guide animals who have passed over.*
>
> *I let him be in deep peace and let him see that when it is his time he can fly like an eagle and that heaven is filled with "pet shops" and treats.*
>
> *This gave him a smile, and he is now surrounded by four angels.*

No emotional bracing could prepare me for this moment. He was too young, only 9-and-a-half years old. In a matter of minutes, my feelings ranged from incredible sadness to guilt and then gratitude. I was remembering how much joy and love he had given me. He had changed my life forever. I had so much to thank him for. The least I could do for him was to help him transition peacefully.

I called the vet's office. In the past, they had warned that Indi's extremely enlarged heart could back up water into his lungs causing him to drown in his own fluids quickly. This would be an agonizing death. The vet recommended that we take Indi to the hospital straight away if he showed any signs of distress in breathing. Although they were willing to accommodate us, I hoped that Indi would pass peacefully at home.

For the last 36 hours of his life, I didn't leave Indi's side, nor did I sleep. Indi didn't have much time left and I wanted to be fully awake for his remaining hours. He rarely moved and his eyes were barely open. I made sure he could always feel my hand or my body to assure him that I was with him. Although he chose not to eat or drink, I would wet his lips with drops of water every now and then made sure he was neither too hot nor cold. He was so weak, that when doing his business, he required my support. Even carrying him home with no energy to spare, his head would droop onto my shoulder.

I could tell that his life was ebbing, but there were still no visible signs of pain. His breathing remained calm and slow. We laid together for hours, him nestled on my chest so he could hear my heartbeat and feel my love.

In a matter of days or hours, I wouldn't be able to see him or feel him in this physical world anymore. I wanted to remember everything about him. Over and over, I told him how much I loved him and that he didn't have to worry about me. I knew he was listening.

Though, when morning came, nothing had changed.

For the longest time, I had hoped for a miraculous recovery. Sometimes I wished I could be sick for him, and in exchange he could have gained some years. Before Indi's illness, I had never practiced a religion. But now I prayed for a peaceful transition for Indi; one without suffering. I focused only on that image. In the afternoon, I closed my eyes and saw Indi playing with a beautiful butterfly, surrounded by nature. He looked so happy and free from this fragile body he was about to leave.

Knowing butterflies are the symbol of transition, both of us knew the moment was getting closer.

That night, my husband and I were together with Indi in the living room. At 10 pm, I got up to prepare the bed for Indi and myself in our second bedroom. I left Indi with my husband for about 10 minutes. Yet, when I came out to the living room again, Indi was sitting upright, staring at me. His big brown eyes were shiny and alert for the first time in two days. My husband told me that he stood up as soon as I left his sight and had been waiting for me in that position. I was surprised by his strength. He hadn't been able to stand on his own for the last 48 hours.

This gave me a sliver of hope. But as soon as I held him, it melted away. His body felt empty. I laid him down on the bed, stroking his back gently.

"I love you Indi. Thank you for all you have given me. Your time was too short. But I know that you are ready. I will be okay. Don't worry about me. I will be with you until the time comes. I will always remember you, my love, my greatest teacher." All the while, I visualized his peaceful passing.

Around 11 pm, I received an email from Christina. She had been in communication with Indi a few times over the previous days. When she connected this time, it felt as if he was already gone. I looked at him and remembered how vibrant he had looked just minutes before, even though it was brief. For the first time, maybe Christina was wrong. I wanted her to be wrong. I didn't reply immediately.

Instead, I placed my hand on Indi's heart. It felt stable. With my eyes fixed on his, I continued to pray.

Suddenly, there was a change in his heartbeat. As it went from palpable to waning, mine pounded harder.

I couldn't believe this was happening so quickly. Instinctually, I started to countdown in my head, 10, 9, 8, 7, 6 ....

At the last beat of his heart, he opened his eyes wide and looked directly at me. He then slowly and deliberately raised his head pausing to say a final goodbye before looking up to the sky. It appeared that the spirit was now leaving his body. Then his head fell gracefully back onto the pillow.

My hand still rested on his heart, but there was no heartbeat. I was stunned by what I had just witnessed. He was gone. I sat there in disbelief having witnessed his final moment. Not a single struggle, not even a last gasp, just peace and surrender.

He wanted me to understand that there is nothing to fear in life—not even death. This was my Duru's last act of love.

Below is the email I received from Christina about 30 minutes before Indi's death.

> *From: Christina Burki Date: 08-02-2016 10:57 PM (GMT-08:00)*
>
> *Dear Jasmine*
>
> *At the end when I hold him close to me it felt like the white light from above came and brought in a huge stream of peace into his body.*
>
> *It felt like he is gone . . .*
>
> *He feels very weak and feeling not well.*
>
> *He is not in pain but feels not good.*
>
> *He would like to eat nothing in the moment but that you make his lips and tongue wet.*
>
> *He doesn't like it too warm or too cold.*
>
> *When he lays on his side, please put something in his back to support him.*
>
> *A crystal would bring him more peace. I found the crystal, selenite, on the internet.*
>
> *I am not sure if you have that or another crystal that brings this peaceful energy.*
>
> *His answer on your message was "I love you too Jasmine. Even when you think I might not be aware I still feel you stay with me.*
>
> *I need you now and I love you always."*

I send him healing energy so he can do a wee or a poo. I told him that he can do it on the pad.

I told him he has only to focus on him now.

Maybe you could also when he didn't do a wee see him doing it or hold your hands by his belly...mine got really hot.

On my question again if he is suffering of pain the answer was no.

He again wanted a hug of peace and light and he loves candlelight. (I, Jasmine, just lit the light on that night.)

I felt when I had him on close to my stomach and belly that he loves that position.

I can imagine that he might love to be very close to you now.

Maybe you are already asleep. I will soon have a skype session and then will pick up my husband from the airport. I will look tonight around 8 pm again in my emails.

Love to you and a gentle hug to Indi,

Christina

CHAPTER 17
Grief

"Often in times of loss as we reach out for what we have considered to be our strength, we may stumble on our wholeness and our real power."

—RACHEL NAOMI REMEN

For the first few hours after his death, Indi looked as if he was still alive. I even hoped he might wake up, that this whole thing was a dream. But when I held his body, it felt cool and began stiffening, at which point the reality sank in. I stayed up another night, my eyes fixed on Indi. I wanted to remember everything about him before sending him away forever.

The following morning, we took Indi's body to a cremation center. We organized a private cremation service for the next day. I held his cold little body for as long as I could before moving to the cremation room. I was honored to press the fire-starter button. This was my way of loving him and being with him at every step of his life.

The day after we cremated Indi, I woke up at 5 am to

the sound of Indi's crystal pendant hitting his food bowl as he ate. At first, I wondered if I was hallucinating. But a minute later, fully awake in bed, I could still hear the sound very clearly. This happened again the next morning. I stayed in bed listening and was worried it might disappear if I got up. I knew it was Indi. He wanted me to know he was still with us and make sure we were okay. This continued for four straight days.

During this period, I had barely slept. Even after his death, I was waking up in the middle of the night with an overwhelming sense of grief. No words or quantity of tears can describe the excruciating pain in my heart. I thought I was prepared for Indi's death but was overwhelmed by the intensity of my emotions. Every corner where Indi used to rest was now empty. The house was so quiet without his paws clicking around.

Grief came in waves. It didn't matter where I was or what I was doing. Yet it often hit me unexpectedly, whether waiting for a bus, hiking, ordering coffee, sitting on the bench in the park, or talking to a friend about something completely unrelated.

It always seemed that a big chunk of me was missing. The pain was unending.

A week after Indi's passing, I developed shingles. The red blisters formed above my heart. If you've ever had shingles, you'll understand how painful it can be. This forced me to stop everything. I couldn't function. For many days, I slept, woke up to cry, and then fell back to sleep from sheer exhaustion. I didn't know that intense grief from the death of a loved one can increase the risk of heart attack by 21 times.

I wondered whether shingles was a self-defense mechanism. My heart was broken and needed time to mend. But I was continuing with normal activities without giving myself the proper time to mourn. Perhaps getting shingles was my body's way of telling me to let myself feel and heal.

10 days after recovering from shingles, I was finally ready to donate Indi's items to his favorite pet store. Having learned about Indi's passing from one of our neighbors, the store manager, Jessica, greeted me with tears. She was so emotional that she barely managed to say, "I am so sorry about Indi," before bursting into tears. She disappeared into her office and returned with a card prepared by the staff members who knew him.

The card described his essence beautifully: "Indi was a tough little dude. He brought such joy to all that saw him. His spirit and tenacity for life were inspiring. He will be very much missed."

Jessica had had a special relationship with Indi. When Jessica was around, Indi wouldn't leave the store until he'd received a massage from her. I know Indi would have been happy to hear her loving words.

During this time, it was interesting to see how people reacted to my grief. People who have pets usually understand the depth of grief other owners go through. In fact, a few people told me that they grieved the loss of their dog more than the loss of a family member.

Many studies have shown that the death of a beloved pet can be as devastating as the loss of a human significant other.[10] Another study shows that an owner's bond with their dog can be similar to that of a mother and a baby.[11] So, losing a pet, especially a dog, can have the same emotional impact as losing a child. But despite the special bond we have with our pets, there is little to guide us as we grieve for them.

As painful as this period of grief can be, it can also be transformative. Throughout history, major transformations and innovations have come after tragedies, like war. It is the same for individuals. Everybody experiences pain, but in modern societies we act as if pain is something to be suppressed. I think this is because we see happiness as the norm and pain as an aberration to be avoided. But that's not what life is about. Duality exists in everything—like yin and yang, up and down, happiness and sadness. Without duality there is no life. Whether the pain is physical, emotional, or spiritual, it is as much a part of life as happiness is.

What matters is how we handle our painful experiences. If we allow them to distort our views and put up walls to protect ourselves from hurting, we only trap ourselves inside those walls. On the other hand, if we see life as a school and that every life experience is a learning opportunity, it becomes our job to extract lessons from our experiences, especially the painful ones.

---

10 https://www.psychologytoday.com/ca/blog/the-truisms-wellness/201608/why-losing-pet-hurts-so-much
11 https://science.sciencemag.org/content/348/6232/333

Grief is not only the last chapter of love; it's also a sacred, transformative time for us. We do not need to get over it quickly but know it should be honored.

How we process painful experiences defines us. We can harness our pain to become wiser and more resilient. It can even expand our soul's energy and heal us. Or we can suppress our pain, and it will consume us.

CHAPTER 18
Big D and little d

"Dogs come into our lives to teach us about love and loyalty. They depart to teach us about loss. A new dog never replaces an old dog. It merely expands the heart."

—ERICA JONG

Indi and his dad didn't exactly start out on the right paw. When my future husband first learned that I had a dog, he announced that he was a "cat person." And when they met, Indi welcomed him by peeing on the carpet. As he developed a closer relationship with Indi, he justified his affection towards Indi by dubbing Indi a "dat"—a dog who acts like a cat.

Indi and his dad bonded by running together and taking long drives into the Rocky Mountains with Indi strategically positioned on the driver's windowsill. He took pride in Indi's uncharacteristic canine behaviors. He refused to sniff around other dogs' butts, squatted when he peed, never ate off the ground, and was never territorial. In fact, Indi preferred meeting new humans to interacting with other dogs.

He seemed to have a special ability to draw people in. Neighbors always made an effort to acknowledge his royal presence. After a while, my husband recognized this special trait in Indi.

My husband was kind to animals, but he grew up on a farm where animals were subservient and had never formed a deep bond with an animal before Indi. Throughout Indi's illness, we continued to have differences. I valued Indi's life and needs as much as my own or those of any other human being. I believe animals have feelings and have as much right to live on this earth as we do.

This caused conflict between us at times. He valued scientific proof, so had a hard time accepting some of my choices regarding Indi's well-being—like animal communication. We sometimes spent hours talking through our differences.

At one point, I wondered whether we would ever be on the same page.

But several years into our relationship, my husband's interactions with Indi changed. His level of care and connection strengthened. He had always cared for Indi, but originally it felt like it came from a sense of responsibility rather than a genuine, heartfelt connection. Having a dog wasn't his first choice. Indi had been part of the package that came with me. But this was no longer the case. Somewhere along the journey, Indi had become his "little buddy."

The night Indi passed, my husband found me holding

his lifeless body. I had made no sound, not even after Indi's death, because I didn't want to disturb his spirit's transition. However, my husband did not know yet that Indi had left this earth.

He started sobbing uncontrollably. It caught me off guard. Until that moment, I had never realized the impact that Indi had had on him.

I remembered one of the messages Indi had channeled through Christina: "Take daddy with you to do your work when he's ready." It was a curious message; I thought our perspectives on animals were too different for that to be possible.

Then one day, after Indi's death, I understood what Indi meant. Without prompting, my husband expressed his desire to support animal rights in the future. I challenged him "Where did this come from?" He explained that on the farm, animals were caged, mistreated, and ultimately consumed or displayed for our entertainment. Indi had presented the ultimate case for the goodness of animals when treated as equals. Animals are capable of the same feelings we have, yet their voices are rarely respected because of our language differences. We spend more time trying to communicate with tribes lost in the Amazon than we do with the native animals in our midst. And on he went.

I couldn't believe my ears. We were on the same page. He said, "Indi taught me. The littlest was the wisest."

Being able to share the same perspective with my husband

was another step on the road to recovery.

If you think you are too small to create change in your world, let Indi prove you wrong. Years after Indi's death, my husband still gets teary-eyed speaking of Indi. It touches me every time.

When I said to him, "You've changed a lot," he replied, "I felt honored to know Indi."

I can see Indi's little paw print on his dad's heart.

CHAPTER 19
Reflections

"Realize that your world is only a reflection of yourself and stop finding fault with the reflection. Attend to yourself, set yourself right; mentally and emotionally. The physical self will follow automatically."

—SRI NISARGADATTA MAHARAJ

My husband used to joke that he couldn't tell the difference between Indi and me. Professor Richard Wiseman of the University of Hertfordshire, who conducted online research on almost 2,500 people with pets, many lovers of dogs, cats, and even reptiles, found that they shared similar traits with their pets.

"For years, owners have insisted their pets have a unique personality," he writes. "Not only does this work suggest they might be right, it also reveals people's pets are a reflection of themselves."

This is exactly how I felt about Indi. In the later part of his life, I started to think Indi shared more than just my personality traits. It went deeper than that.

Animals are in tune with the energy of their human. They also tend to take on human energy disturbances in an effort to share the burdens.[12] It is not uncommon to see illness being mirrored between the owner and the pet.[13] This is why it is important for some animal healers to work with both the owners and their pets.

I wondered what the study meant for Indi and me. How was Indi's heart condition related to me? Do I have an unknown heart problem?

Some might think that this is far-fetched. It is true that certain breeds are more prone to particular health conditions. However, I accepted him into my life. Since I believe there are no coincidences, sometimes unconsciously, we attract a specific being into our lives.

The animals in our lives are not there by accident.

When Indi first arrived, I was longing for the kind of joy that comes from expressing one's true essence. Instead, I felt trapped by social norms and expectations. I was following the dreadful traditional list of "shoulds".

However, deep inside of my heart, living a conventional life and following a formula for material success felt wrong. But never having a chance to explore my passion growing up, I didn't know what I wanted.

I went through life's motions, fulfilling responsibilities without much joy. I became guarded and had slowly built an invisible wall around my heart. As joy is associated

---

12 https://www.npr.org/sections/health-shots/2019/06/06/729328198/you-may-be-stressing-out-your-dog
13 https://wisdom-magazine.com/Article.aspx/3222/

with the heart, a lack of it impacts the heart's energy. Indi's heart condition wasn't just his alone.

I started to notice more of my reflection in Indi. For example, Indi was a quiet dog. He rarely barked. At first, I wished he would use his voice more often. Then I realized I did the same. I rarely used my voice. He even has a minor delay in hand-eye coordination, just like his human. We were mutually challenged to watch ball games.

As a microcosm of myself, I now see that Indi was showing me the way forward.

This reflection is not just through our pets. It is everywhere and in everything around us—in our job, family, friends, nature, movies, and so on. What we notice and the way we feel about these things are reflections of our inner state. They often reveal the very challenges and the (hidden) patterns we need to overcome in order to heal ourselves.

This is a powerful way to live. By recognizing our surroundings as a reflection of ourselves, we can bring changes into our lives. Instead of seeing that things are happening *to* us, we choose to see that things are happening *for* us. This is how we can live in gratitude—and 'living in gratitude' is the ultimate spiritual practice.

All answers are inside of us. The animals are our messengers.

CHAPTER 20
Journey after the journey

"Trust in yourself whatever life brings you. Don't let an unpleasant experience ruin who you are. Find joy every day. Your heart is your ally. It will guide you to live your life more harmoniously. As I have trusted you, trust your core goodness, and everything will work out beautifully."

—INDI

Beyond just sharing our story, there was a deeper meaning to Indi's encouragement to write. He wanted me to realize that fear can be a great teacher.

While he was unable to fulfill a long life, his grace amidst his health challenge was inspiring. In kind, his courage and unconditional love opened my heart. The intuition and imagination that helped to write this story can be directly attributed to his wisdom.

As a private and introverted person, it is not natural to

share the details of my life with others. I never wrote anything unless it was absolutely required. Labeled as someone who didn't like to write at nine years of age, I avoided picking up a pen at all costs. I didn't want to be judged by others. Therefore, emotionally and mentally, writing this journey was always going to be one of the ultimate challenges, particularly in an adopted language.

Yet, it has also been liberating. It forced me to reflect on my fears and their origins. A lot of fear is learned in early childhood. It hinders us by framing our thoughts around what we don't want, not what might be best for us. We try to control everything to create a "safe and comfortable" environment and limit ourselves according to the smallness of fear.

By facing fear, we are able to discover a reservoir of courage and free ourselves from its shackles.

Every philosophy teaches that the heart's wisdom is undeniable. Embedded in it are our desires, dreams, and purposes. Learning to follow its wisdom can help us confront and transform our fears into growth. Because only our heart knows what is uniquely true for each of us regardless of other people's opinions. Listening to our heart means trusting ourselves despite our fears.

While writing this story, I let go of many layers of fear. Indi's inspiration has kept me motivated and the shift has been profound.

We can achieve many things during life's journey, but learning and personal evolution matter more than the goals themselves. This can only happen when we trust and follow our hearts. When we are filled with joy and happiness, we will touch so many more hearts—just like my Duru.

A LETTER TO INDI

Hi Indi,

Many years have passed since you left us. Yet, not a day has passed by when I didn't feel your presence. Our neighbors still remember you, and your dad still pines for his royal-pooper-scooper days. I miss your polite little tap on my arm when your patience ran out.

I want to tell you that the inspiration you gave me to write this story also gave inspiration for another book written by your dad, *"The Investing Oasis"*.

I want to thank you for pushing me out of my comfort zone to share this story. You have helped me to grow and heal in more ways than I thought possible.

Thank you for your undying, unconditional love. I had never experienced such love before you. It has been a source of personal transformation for at least two humans, but hopefully more—including the many readers of this book.

Thank you for coming into my life. I feel very lucky to have experienced our journey and intend to honor it every day. My life will never be the same because of you.

I feel that sharing your story is just the beginning. It will be my journey to walk a similar path—to live a life filled with joy and share it with the world.

I hope you are still having lots of fun chasing, but not catching, squirrels wherever you are.

Until we meet again, you will be forever in my heart.

Love,
Jasmine

FURTHER INSIGHTS

The following insights were not included in the story. What has created the most meaningful change in my life is repetitively feeding my mind with quality information.

Like some of you, I knew most of this before. But it didn't necessarily translate into actions. Repetition brings awareness to the deeper meaning of the same information. But more importantly, repetition helps this knowledge to become part of you and then you will be able to apply it in daily life.

A. Critical thinking

> *"Unthinking respect for authority is the greatest enemy of truth."*
>
> —ALBERT EINSTEIN

In the documentary *I Am*, the Dalai Lama is asked: What is the most important meditation we can do now?

His answer was, "Critical thinking followed by action. Discern what your world is. Know the plot of your life of this human drama and figure out where your talents might fit in to make a better world."

Rather than using our critical thinking abilities, we tend to follow norms and don't question the most obvious things. At times, we act a certain way without realizing that our perceptions are preconditioned. We also tend to depend on authority figures or media for guidance, just like I accepted the first vet's recommendation on kibble without an ounce of doubt. He was the expert, and I was not—or so I thought.

If we look closely, this kind of blind acceptance exists in many aspects of life. We see this clearly in politics and religion. The ultimate danger of blind faith is extreme fundamentalism, which can result in everything from oppression of individuals to acts of terrorism around the world.

More people are now re-evaluating their lives and their decisions. Critical thinking can help us bring about changes in dated and destructive practices. No matter how insignificant we believe our role is, every decision deserves self-reflection and mindfulness.

B. The power of thoughts and prayers

"Thought is a thing that affects other things. Thought generates its own palpable energy that you can use to improve your life, to help others around you, and to change the world."

—Lynn McTaggart

Experts estimate we have 50,000 or more thoughts per day. How many are we aware of and how many are we using intentionally, to move ourselves and the world around us in the direction we wish to see?

In the 1990s, Dr. Masaru Emoto conducted experiments that demonstrated the physical effects of prayers, thoughts, and music on the crystalline structure of water. He discovered that the crystalline structure of water changed from an ugly shape to a more beautiful structure when it was exposed to positive emotions and focused thoughts, such as prayer.[14] As water makes up 60-70 percent of the human body and more than 70 percent of our planet, the implication of this study on our health and the earth is significant.

One of the most famous studies on prayer was published in 1988 by Dr. Randolph Byrd.[15] This study involved 393 patients in the coronary care unit in San Francisco General Hospital. The results of this double-blind study showed that the prayed-for patients did significantly better, experiencing fewer symptoms and requiring fewer drugs and medical intervention. These are only a few studies that demonstrate the power of our thoughts and prayers.

When it comes to prayer, the way we pray is also important. Many prayers are based in fear, or a feeling that something is lacking in our lives. But this is an ineffective way to pray. As Gregg Braden writes in *Secrets of the Lost Mode of Prayer*, we have to use the language the universe understands when we pray. For the universe to understand our prayer, we must embody the quality of the thing we pray for—to become the frequency of our desire through our feelings and emotions. In Braden's words, "Feel as if our prayer has already been answered, rather than feeling powerless and needing to ask for help

---

14 The hidden messages in water, Masaru Emoto, 2005
15 https://pubmed.ncbi.nlm.nih.gov/3393937/

from a higher source." Our feelings and emotions are the language the universe understands.

C. Conscious self-care

"Self-care is never a selfish act—it is simply good stewardship of the only gift I have, the gift I was put on earth to offer others. Anytime we can listen to true self and give the care it requires, we do it not only for ourselves, but for the many others whose lives we touch.

—PARKER PALMER

Through many communications with Christina, Indi had one persistent message for me: "Take better care of yourself."

It is a common misconception that love means sacrificing our own needs. Some people think tending to our needs is selfish and feel guilty about it. But consider the airplane oxygen mask analogy: We need to put on our oxygen masks first before helping others.

When other people's agendas become the driving force in our lives, we can become emotionally dependent on them. Our happiness is contingent upon others' moods and opinions. Some people expect us to make them happy instead of taking responsibility for their own emotional states.

When we habitually care about how others think and feel, it becomes easy to neglect our own needs. Energy leaves and is not replenished, which creates internal disharmony.

We may feel resentful or angry—'dried out' on a soul level.

I believe the most important aspect of self-care is learning to say 'no'. From my experience, the first few times are the hardest. But after the initial uncomfortable moments, you get used to it, and so do the other parties involved. This action alone is very empowering and creates more time to care for ourselves.

We can refuel through conscious and deliberate self-care. This will help us to better tune-in and help others without being exhausted by their drama and emotional burdens.

Self-care doesn't have to be time consuming at all. But everything should be under consideration, including nourishment, sleep, exercise, friends, et al. It is about learning to listen to our body's signals. Simple, everyday choices can be acts of self-care.

Most importantly, this is about loving ourselves and prioritizing our needs. When we are filled with love, we can love others more. As we start to take care of ourselves more consciously, we will find everything seems to flow effortlessly.

D. Breathing and meditation

"If you are not breathing fully, you cannot live fully. And every change that is going to happen is going to happen through the change in your breathing."

—OSHO

Watching Indi gasp for air when his heart failed, all I wanted was for him to breathe normally again. I was immensely relieved when his breathing returned to normal. During the last two days of Indi's life, I could feel the life leaving his fragile body with every breath.

Through this heartache, I began to appreciate how precious breath is. I realized that what matters most in our lives are things that are already available to us—like air and the ability to breathe.

I developed a habit of deep breathing/meditating as a by-product of Indi's heart condition. I would say breathwork and meditation have brought the most powerful change to my life, beyond what any healing modalities could bring.

We can't separate breath from life. Therefore, our breathing patterns reflect our life patterns, revealing how we react and process life experiences. When the breath is somehow inhibited or broken, aspects of our life might be inhibited or broken. Similarly, a sense of unease in us will show up in our breath. Consequently, if we change our breath, we can change our lives.

Breathwork and meditation are two sides of the same coin. The Tibetan word for "meditate" is *'gom'*, which means "to familiarize." Meditation is about familiarizing ourselves with our minds. Meditation helps relax the mind and helps us recognize its attachments, judgments, and narratives. It helps us to see what is preventing us from living fully.

Meditation is also the fastest way to become familiarized with our authentic self. Our authentic self knows that our own harmony contributes to harmony in the universe. It can guide us to live a harmonious and deeply fulfilling life.

Therefore, meditation is not a supplementary, occasional activity for stress relief. It is a way of living. Our animals show us how natural it is to meditate. When you see a dog and a cat sitting under the sun, watch how they instinctively know to be still.

There is no one way to meditate. Try different forms, find the form you like, and learn to appreciate your breath every day.

E. The gift of sensitivity

"Sensitive people should be treasured. They love deeply and think deeply about life. They are loyal, honest, and true. The simple things sometimes mean the most to them. They don't need to change or harden. Their purity makes them who they are."

—KRISTEN BUTLER

Indi was a very sensitive dog. One time, while we were living in Dallas, I left him for three days at a reputable overnight facility. The day after I picked him up, he had diarrhea with a little bit of blood, which can happen to dogs when they are under prolonged stress. The vet guessed that Indi was probably stressed about being in a kennel, given his quiet personality. Indeed, he didn't necessarily enjoy playing with other dogs or getting petted by random people. He was very selective about who he spent time with.

Indi seemed to know he was sensitive to subtleties in his surroundings. He preferred to observe a while before jumping in. Because of this, some people thought he was shy and timid. I don't believe that; I think he just knew his preferences and boundaries.

Having a sensitivity to one's surroundings is not unique to animals. Chances are that you are sensitive—or maybe highly sensitive like Indi and me. Otherwise, you wouldn't have picked up this book.

A "highly sensitive person" (HSP) is a term introduced by Dr. Elaine N. Aron, the author of *The Highly Sensitive Person*. According to her research, highly sensitive people have biologically different nervous systems, which process and analyze sensory data at a deeper level. This, in turn, helps them notice details and see subtleties that others miss.

HSPs are often labeled as shy or introverted. These are not considered positive traits. Toughness and extroversion are perceived as positive traits; sensitivity gets little to no respect. This is why many highly sensitive people suffer from low self-esteem and self-worth. We have to remember that we are not just physical beings, we are also emotional beings.

Our sensitivity is meant to benefit, not overwhelm, us. This heightened awareness can help to bring balance to our world. It can be a source of wisdom and truth.

The most critical thing you can do is to embrace sensitivity as a gift. Start treating your sensitivity as a unique trait—a strength.

Setting healthy boundaries is important for sensitive people, because we tend to be easily influenced by other people's energy. The company you keep is vital to your well-being. If you have difficulty finding people who respect your sensitivity, you may need to spend time alone for a while, as I did. That is another important aspect of nurturing your sensitivity.

Lastly, surround yourself with nature as much as you can. We don't need to be plugged-in 24/7. Hugging trees and earthing (also known as grounding) are all good ways to sync ourselves with nature.

F. Beneficial modalities

There are four modalities I frequently used for Indi. I chose these four because I used them myself and was familiar with them. I occasionally engaged other modalities such as reiki and shamanism. They are also helpful, but again, I believe it is important to find a properly trained practitioner who is the right fit for you and your animal.

Acupuncture

I gave Indi regular acupuncture treatments in the beginning. Since I am trained to treat humans only, I purchased a book about acupuncture points in animals.

Acupuncture is a 3,000-year-old system that can treat and prevent illness. It's the main component of Traditional Chinese Medicine (TCM). All beings have life energy called *qi* (pronounced "chee"). This energy flows through the body along pathways called meridians. When the flow of energy becomes blocked, we experience pain, sickness, and other imbalances. Acupuncture restores harmony to the body through the insertion of fine needles at specific points chosen in accordance with a patient's individual needs and Traditional Chinese Medicine diagnosis.

I can't comment on acupuncture services provided by vets because I don't have experience with them. What I know through some people who have engaged in acupuncture for their pets is that it seems to be hit or miss. If you are interested in acupuncture for your pet, find a qualified practitioner and ask them about their training. If you feel comfortable with the practitioner, try two to three sessions to see if it helps your animal.

BodyTalk

Later on, I used more BodyTalk than acupuncture since Indi had a better response to it.

BodyTalk was developed in the 1990s by Dr. John Veltheim, an Australian chiropractor, acupuncturist, philosopher, and teacher. The system combines Western medical principles, acupuncture, applied kinesiology, and quantum physics. BodyTalk is a simple, non-invasive modality based on the belief that healing happens when all the parts and systems of the body are able to communicate with each other. Our bodies are like complex ecosystems. As such, they need to strike a delicate balance. There must be communication among physiological functions, emotional and mental factors, and environmental and genetic influences.

However, internal or external stress can cause communication among these elements to break down, resulting in discomfort and disease. These symptoms are the tip of the iceberg. BodyTalk identifies underlying causes and uses a light tapping technique to restore intercellular communication that invokes the body's own inherent healing power. This can be done in person or from a distance. You can find more information about this modality on their website, *www.bodytalksystem.com*.

Crystals

I was introduced to the healing power of crystals and their benefits to animals through a workshop provided by a local healer in Vancouver. After taking a workshop on crystals, I decided to incorporate crystals into Indi's care regime, as well as my own.

For Indi, I ordered a crystal necklace to support his energy. That's how I met Tamara, who made the necklace for Indi. When Indi saw the necklace for the first time, he wagged his tail really fast, as if he recognized its benefits. He loved his necklace and wore it until he passed.

The energetic frequency of crystals is among the highest vibrational frequencies on Earth. Because of this orderliness, crystals emit consistent energy that balances and transforms disharmonic energy. Crystals affect us by subtly realigning energy through vibration, so that our energy matches that of the highly balanced crystal.

You can find the benefits of crystals for common conditions in books or online. Just make sure you energetically cleanse the crystals before your first use and after each use. My go-to cleansing method is smudging the crystals using sage. There are other cleansing methods, but I find smudging with sage works best for me. To charge crystals, place them near a window where they can be exposed to direct sunlight or moonlight for 24 hours. I charge them during the full moon.

To receive maximum benefits from crystal healing, you should be properly trained or be treated by qualified practitioners.

Music therapy

Music is a big part of my practice because I have noticed its calming effects on my clients. I always played soothing music for Indi, especially when I left him alone at home.

Music has been used for healing for many years across different cultures. One study showed that music could help stimulate neurological functions in humans after a stroke.[16] There aren't many studies about the impact of music on animals yet, but I believe the impact is similar. There are many YouTube videos on how animals are drawn to beautiful music. They respond in various ways: singing, howling, or sleeping, depending on the tune.

Deborah Wells, a psychologist from Queen's University, Belfast, found that classical music had a calming effect on shelter dogs. Another study by a veterinary neurologist, Susan Wagner, showed that classical music lowered the heart rate and brain activity of dogs.[17]

---

16 https://www.sciencedaily.com/releases/2008/02/080219203554.htm
17 https://www.entirelypets.com/how-does-music-affect-your-dog.html

Indi responded well to music. He often fell asleep faster with soothing music; on those days, I'd find him looking pretty chill when I came home. He often went to bed as soon as I played the relaxing music.

A sound healer, Tom Keyon, says, "The vibratory nature of sound and music creates a language which the body and mind understand."[18] Gentle music sends vibrations that can have positive physiological impacts on animals.

For Indi, I would play gentle flute or harp music that I use at my clinic and sometimes recordings of the sound of the forest because he loved being in the forest. I found many free, soothing songs for animals on YouTube that were helpful as well.

G. Other tips

Dangers of a collar

When Indi was a little puppy, my ex-husband bought a metal collar to train him, based on recommendations from other dog owners. This collar, or choke chain, was made of metal links and was designed to control the dog by tightening around its neck when it misbehaved. I never liked the idea of a choke chain. But others assured me it was safe. I was told that a dog's neck is strong enough to withstand this type of collar.

Indi wore the choke chain when he was in training at home for the first three months. Thankfully, he didn't need much training and wore a regular collar when we

---

18 Theoretical Constructs of ABR Technology by Tom Kenyon, M.A

went out for a walk. Indi was a puller. He pulled the leash when walking. I was horrified when I learned the potential harm that collars can cause in dogs. I wondered whether using the collar accelerated Indi's heart problem.

Based on my readings, given that dogs' neck anatomy is similar to humans, using a collar can cause neck injuries. Collars can also contribute to other kinds of disease, such as hypothyroidism, digestive issues, lung and heart problem, and eye and ear issues[19].

In Traditional Chinese Medicine, a number of major meridians run through the neck to the head. Energy and blood flow through the body along meridians, so I can imagine how strong jerks and repeated pulling could cause a blockage of energy and blood flow, like whiplash. If not addressed, these injuries can cause other harmful conditions over time.

Using a harness for a dog instead of a collar or a chain could benefit the dog's long-term health. There are various types of no-pull dog harnesses available to prevent dogs from pulling on the leash. I hope one day collars will come with warning signs so dog owners can make an educated decision.

Natural antibiotics for your dog

The Human Microbiome Project (2007-2016) demonstrated that the human body is a microbial ecosystem. Some 100 trillion micro-organisms, including bacteria, viruses and fungi, live in and on a human body. Their

---

[19] https://peterdobias.com/blogs/blog/11015137-choke-prong-and-shock-collars-can-irreversibly-damage-your-dog

diversity is key to our health, as well as the health of our animals.

Since antibiotics diminish the biodiversity of our microbial ecosystems, we should be cautious of using antibiotics on animals. These are some of the natural products I used for Indi and myself that are less damaging to healthy microbiomes.

Disclaimer: These were the solutions that worked for my household. I am not a doctor or a veterinarian. I am providing this information for educational purposes only. Always seek the advice of your vet or another qualified healthcare provider for any questions you have regarding a medical condition, and before undertaking any diet or other health-related program.

1. Oil of oregano

The health benefits of oregano oil come from carvacrol and thymol, powerful phenols that can kill harmful bacteria and microbes without any negative impact. Many farmers use oil of oregano instead of antibiotics to keep their livestock safe from disease. Oregano oil has antibacterial, anti-fungal, antiviral, and anti-parasitic properties.

Apply oil of oregano orally or topically. *The key is that you need to dilute the oregano oil before giving it to your dog.* You can mix two to three drops into a teaspoon of coconut oil for oral intake, or you can mix one drop of oregano oil with a teaspoon of coconut oil for topical use.

2. Colloidal silver

Colloidal silver is called a liquid antibiotic and has anti-fungal and antiviral properties. It can be used as a topical solution for cuts and all kinds of infections. Its particles are so tiny that they are thought to penetrate cells and kill unwanted pathogens. Since colloidal silver doesn't sting or burn, it can be used directly on sensitive areas. I used colloidal silver topically only. If it is taken orally, it still reduces good bacteria just like antibiotics (albeit with less negative effect) and it may interact with other medications. If you choose to use it orally, take prebiotics and probiotics to build up good bacteria again or consult with your healthcare provider. The quality of colloidal silver varies, so do your research or get a recommendation from your healthcare provider.

3. Honey and manuka honey

Honey is antibacterial because it contains a significant amount of antiseptic hydrogen peroxide. Manuka honey from New Zealand and Australia is especially noteworthy because it contains other antibacterial components besides hydrogen peroxide. This makes manuka honey a powerful and stable agent. Manuka honey is great for cuts and wounds as a topical antiseptic. It is also helpful for digestive issues like gastritis. It is antibiotic, anti-fungal, and antiviral.

Manuka honey is an effective remedy for kennel cough, ringworm, and other conditions.

UMF stands for Unique Manuka Factor. A higher number

means more therapeutic benefits. Look for one with at least UMF10+.

Other types of honey can be easily purchased from a variety of sources. Fresh, unprocessed varieties can generally be expected to have better effects. Find trusted local suppliers at farmers' markets or other local retailers.

Caution: Honey shouldn't be given to dogs with diabetes or puppies under one year old.

Dangers of summer heat (especially for those with a heart condition)

The Five Element theory in Chinese medicine is a framework that categorizes all natural phenomena into five patterns: wood, fire, earth, metal, and water. They represent the movements and frequencies in our bodies and in nature. According to this theory, the heart is associated with the element of fire. The summertime and heat are examples of the fire element. Exposure to extreme weather conditions can impact the balance in our body. Therefore, the hot summer season can negatively affect heart health for dogs or humans with heart conditions.

According to a research article published in *Environmental Health Perspective* in August 2012, heat and heart disease are not a good combination. This study found that adults with an existing heart condition are vulnerable to heat-related deaths. It also says that people with a history of heart failure are more vulnerable to recurring heart failure during hot weather.

I believe this study and the Five Element principle also apply to animals, even those that do not have heart conditions. The negative impact of heat was obvious for Indi, who struggled on hot days because of his weak heart. His breathing rate was higher than his usual range, and he would pant quite often to cool himself down.

We went out only during the cool mornings and evenings, before sunrise and after sunset. When he had to go out during the day, I always took him to shady areas. I also provided a cooling mat for him to lie on at home. The coolest spot in our home was the bathroom, so I left the bathroom door open at all times for him.

I also implemented some Traditional Chinese Medicine dietary principles to help Indi stay cool during the summer. According to Chinese Medicine, foods can either warm or cool the body. For example, chicken and lamb are warm foods, so I avoided these meats for Indi during the summertime. I also added cooling vegetables and fruits, such as cucumber, celery, and watermelon (no seeds) to his diet.

Dogs do sweat a little bit, but they cool down through panting. When the air is hot, it is difficult for dogs to cool down. Taking dogs out for a walk or run in hot weather could be dangerous for them. If your dogs are old or have some kind of serious condition like a heart problem, it is important to prevent them from overheating.

MEMORIES OF INDI FROM CHRISTINA

It is an honor to write a couple of memories here. I still get tears in my eyes when I write or think of Indi. He has touched me in a profound way—in a way that is hard to put into words. I feel that he truly touched my heart and soul and still does.

Indi was a very special being. I understand why Jasmine calls him her Duru. He was a dog filled with love for others and shared his love freely with many human beings. Jasmine once asked Indi what he wanted to pass on through his beautiful big brown eyes. He replied: *"Love, love, and love and let the people be deeply touched by my energy. It lets them see even when your body is not strong and healthy, your inner energy is your essence. I will spread love as long as I can. Jasmine will get the most, but I wish I can touch more people's hearts. I am like the lighter for the candle. I feel that when people see me again, they also send me love"*.

Once, when Jasmine and I had nearly lost the trust in our process, Indi told me not to give up. He still trusted the process, and he urged us to trust in it. He was an inspiration for both of us.

Indi, Jasmine, and I partnered in an amazing way: paw in hand and hand in hand. It didn't feel like work. Indi told me what he needed and preferred. I let Jasmine know, and she provided it to him.

I also worked with healing energy, music and tailor-made meditations for him. In our last meditation, I asked that Indi think about leaving his body and flying towards the sky. So he did. It was a difficult last talk with Indi, but it felt right.

Indi told Jasmine to be prouder, to shine her light brighter, and that he would wait until he saw her inner and outer growth happen before passing over. I know he is so proud of you, Jasmine!

He is still around you, Jasmine, and your husband. He expressed his love for your husband in communications and is thankful for their connection and the connection he had with other human beings.

Like Jasmine mentioned, Indi brought love everywhere he went. And that is what he always told me—that he brings in joy. What Indi teaches us is to be present in the moment.

In this time of uncertainty due to Covid-19, I feel that Indi's message of hope and love is so essential to take in deeply. He has a precious place in my heart and I will never forget him.

NOTES

Bruce H. Lipton, Ph.D. (2008). The biology of belief. Carlsbad, CA: Hay House, Inc.

David Wilcock (2016). The synchronicity key. New York, NY: Dutton.

Dawson Church (2014). The genie in your genes. Sant Rosa, CA: Energy Psychology Press.

Deepak Chopra (1990). Quantum healing: exploring the frontiers of mind/body medicine. New York, NY: Bantam.

Doc Childre, Howard Martin, Deborah Rozman and Rollin Mccraty (2016). Heart intelligence. Waterfront Digital Press.

Duane Elgin (2009). The living universe. San Francisco, CA: Berrett-Koehler Publishers, Inc.

Eckhart Tolle (1997). The power of now. Vancouver, BC: Namaste Publishing.

Elaine N. Aron, Ph.D. (1996). The highly sensitive person. New York, NY: Carol Publishing Group.

Elisabeth Kübler-Ross & David Kessler (2000). Life lessons. New York, NY: Scribner.

Fritjof Capra (2010). The tao of physics. Boulder, CO: Shambhala Publications.

Gregg Braden (2017). Human by design. Hay House.

Gregg Braden (2006). Secrets of the lost mode of prayer. Hay House.

Jean Houston (2002). Mystical dogs. Makawao, Maui, HI: Inner Ocean Publishing.

Joe Dispenza (2017). Becoming Supernatural. Carlsbad, CA: Hay House.

John Veltheim & Sylvia Muiznieks (2013) BodyTalk fundamentals. Sarasota, FL: PaRama LLC.

Larry Dossey, M.D. (2006). The extraordinary healing power of ordinary things, New York, NY: Three Rivers Press.

Lynne Taggart (2008). The intention experiment: using your thoughts to change your life and the world. New York, NY: Atria Trade Paperbacks.

Masaru Emoto (2005). The hidden messages in water. New York, NY: Atria Books.

Richard Bartlett (2010). The physics of miracles. New York, NY: Atria Trade Paperbacks.

WEB REFERENCES

https://thetruthaboutcancer.com/emotional-clearing/

http://www.thedrakecenter.com/materials/heart-disease-dogs

http://dogtime.com/dog-health/general/317-heart-disease#iP4IDJi82MOXb84G.99

http://www.whatthebleep.com/water-crystals/

http://www.richardwiseman.com/resources/petspress.pdf

https://dogtime.com/dog-health/general/21223-music-therapy-for-dogs-and-cats

https://www.dogsnaturallymagazine.com/three-natural-antibiotics-for-your-dog/

http://www.pethealthnetwork.com/dog-health/dog-checkups-preventive-care/our-top-10-summer-safety-tips-dogs

Brittany!

You have a beautiful & strong soul. Trust your SELF, and trust more when in doubt. Everything will work out beautifully for you!

Love
Jasmine

Manufactured by Amazon.ca
Bolton, ON